In the Image of God

In the Image of God

Rev. Robert S. Smith

Yuganta Press

ISBN 0-938999-01-X
Library of Congress Catalog Card Number 86-51607

First Edition

Yuganta Press
6 Rushmore Circle
Stamford, CT 06905

Preface

This book is an invitation to the reader to join in a conversation which has continued over many years. A wise and very human monk once said to me that the things between God and us can be truthfully spoken about only in the way that friends talk to friends. I have tried to write down a partial record of such talk which has taken place among a group of Catholic Christians who came together to celebrate the Eucharist at a university on Long Island.

In the conversation of friends two things play an essential part: time and silence. Their talk is full of memories which slowly change and grow and echo in the words spoken and heard in the present. And friends are always aware of the future which is being shaped by their being together now.

Silence is not only the comfortable expression of affection and acceptance, but it is the rich soil in which this special kind of talk is nourished. If you read

*these notes of conversations about the
human as a creation in the image of
God, I would hope that you would bring
to them memories from the stories of lives
you have been part of and that silence in
which men and women and God can
recognize each other's voice.*

*For those of you who have been my
friends over these many years, I hope this
small book will be a new way for us to be
with each other in the presence of God's
word. For those who might be joining
this conversation for the first time, I hope
this book will help you to discover something more of the depths of your own
self....*

In the Image of God.

Being a believer is a way of being a human being, not a way of escaping being human. Rather than a way of avoiding the dark and troublesome parts of life, belief is a way of living them. Indeed, as we realize more and more in our day, being a believer is one way among many possible ways of being human. ✻ One very helpful way to think about human life is to see it as an interior journey or, even more subtly, as a collection of parallel and intersecting journeys. The center to which many of these journeys return, the place through which the inner dynamisms of prayer and liturgical experience pass and repass, is the moment of our own baptism. Over and over we come back to it in our life with more experience, greater vulnerability, maybe more wisdom and depth, more sense of what human life is about. ✻ We come round and round to this extraordinary event that touched most of us, as very many of the most definitive events in our life did touch us, before we were masters of our own life. We come back not only with human experience, but with a growing sensitivity that comes from the experience of other people who have been seized by God in this way, plunged into the mystery of Christ as we have been. We come back to it over and over again wondering what happened to us. ✍ Like people who have been through a war, or Americans who have lived through the Great Depression, or someone who knew an extraordinary love affair, we know that in some way this is the source of our life and our destiny. We go back to discover who we are now, the limits of our being now, the shape of our own faith. ✍ The story that's told in the Gospel (Lk 4: 1–13) this morning is crucial for our living these journeys which are the stuff of our life, the texture of our freedom. Lent is meant to be an intense time of living our own belief, of becoming more freely human. If we are to become more human in the way of a believer, we must discover what are our real temptations. What answer could you give right now to the question, "What is the central temptation of your life?" ✍ The crucial thing in Lent is the discovery that you're a sinner. And that's crucial because discovering you're a sinner is the

only way to discover that you are not simply burdened by guilt. To discover you're
a sinner is to discover that you're guilty in
the presence of love, not just guilty alone,
not just trapped in your own history alone.
✒ Guilt. Let me just run through this
very quickly. Guilt has to do with ethical
life. Anybody who has lived long enough
to reach puberty knows that you do things
wrong. Everybody knows that there are
some things you have failed at, that you're
guilty, that you've done things that you
shouldn't do, that you've lost opportunities that you should have taken advantage
of. Everybody knows that. What kind of a
person would you be if you couldn't face
the fact? ✒ You want to know what
you're doing wrong because you know that
if you don't know what you're doing
wrong you're just trapped in it. The discovery of guilt, however, leaves you only
at a certain level. At the level of ethics.
There are things you do you shouldn't
do. There are things you're not doing that
you should do and you want to find out
what they are so that you can be liberated
from the dark sides of your own history.
If you don't find out what they are you're

just trapped at that level. Everybody knows that. Guilt is not such a terrible thing.

🖋 But you can discover yourself as a sinner only when you become aware of the presence of God. Sin means that the things you've done or haven't done, that the opportunities you've missed are an abuse of gifts. You can say, "I'm a sinner," only when you're aware of the giver of the gifts, whatever the awareness is, very low, very intense. And if you're aware of Him, then you have to be aware of Him as He really is, and that's as one loving you and forgiving you. You can have a sense of sin only if you're aware of yourself as forgiven. If you're aware of yourself simply as guilty then you haven't yet arrived at a sense of sin because you're thinking about your own life apart from God.

🖋 Now, one of the crucial ways to that awareness of sin, and therefore, to the awareness of the Father, is through becoming really conscious of your temptations. When you were baptized you were liberated. It's easy to say from what: liberated from death. But what were you liberated into? Freed into? Everybody talks about *Roots* these days—the most crucial part of that story is what happened to the American slaves when they were freed, into what kind of world they were freed, not only from what. ✒ The image of Jesus in the desert, the completely liberated man—what is He liberated into? Turmoil. He's liberated into a desert of temptation, continual encounter with the adversary. Or He's liberated into a life that's deeper than the life He knew before. ✒ In the same way, you're liberated into a life that has more at risk. There are all sorts of analogies to this. If you just get out of some neurosis that is binding you, what are you liberated into? A life without trouble? No. You're probably liberated into a tougher life than the one you have known. ✒ Everybody knows that the beds that we lie in hide traps that await us; where we are comfortable are the places where we are not free. This is similar to what happens in the religious life. When you really start being with somebody else, life doesn't get simpler, it gets more complicated. ✒ To be baptized is not to be put into a world where there are no temptations, but to be put into a world where there are temptations that really count for some-

5

thing. You're tempted when you're really alive. If you could succeed in staying asleep all day and night, you'd have no temptations. Once you wake up they start, because once you wake up you're going somewhere. You're moving through something. 🖋 Temptation means any experience, any dimension of your life in which you are at stake. That is, when you're on the other side of it you'll be inevitably different. You'll be better or worse, be more alive or less alive. 🖋 There are dimensions of my own being which are for me now temptations. They're the places where I am at stake. 🖋 The temptations of Jesus that are summarized here, all of the scholars say, are rooted in a lot of different things that happened in His life. Luke organizes them according to a certain theology. For Luke, the whole life of Jesus is a journey up to Jerusalem, which should be a journey toward recognition and love, but which turns out to be a journey of failure and rejection. The temptations are the shape of that journey. 🖋 They're all temptations which He had to pass through because He had to discover what it meant for Him to be the

Messiah. He had to discover the way in which God and human beings were going to meet and be transformed into some kind of common life. ✒ And what is in the back of Luke's mind is that the only way to this, which Jesus finally discovers too, is the way of simplicity and vulnerability. A way of a radical faith that works itself out in apparent weakness. If you're really the Messiah, show it, make it look like God, find your own strength in Him, do something spectacular, meet people at the level they're ready to be met at. And all those things will not do. ✒ What does this mean in day-to-day terms? We have no idea. We have no idea what this meant between Him and one or two other people He met, or crowds of people, or what it was like for Him when He was all alone or between Him and His family. ✒ But one of the things you recognize in Jesus is that there's not just a kind of frenzy and hopelessness and despair, but there is always struggle. There is always the sense that something really crucial is at stake. Filled with the Spirit, led by the Spirit into the desert, the place filled with the adversary, the place filled with conflict

where for forty days He's at the test. ✒
To know that you were baptized, to be
reminded that you have been baptized,
means that you have been liberated somewhere into that kind of conflict. Somewhere in your life now there is the same
sort of temptation going on because you
are now alive enough to face the temptation of questions about your being loved
by God. The journey of faith is in part,
and crucially, becoming aware of where
your true self is at risk in this way. ✒
What do you know now of your own destiny? How vaguely or clearly would you
say you are called to live? What's the story
of your own life now? In the light of that,
against that horizon, where is your desert
where you have to grapple with the de-
mon adversaries? ✒ When the temptation was over, Jesus was still in the desert
because that's the real place of meeting—
it's the real place of growth, the place
where you are at stake. In the light of this
story now, in our common silence, which
is another kind of desert, let yourself be
led by the Spirit. Become even a little aware
of the enormous dignity and importance
of your life and of what is at stake.

At the heart of Christian religious experience there is a paradox which brings us into the presence of the Holy One whom Jesus called Father. The paradox is that, for Christians, the experience of God becomes *identical with* human experience. It is *not* a movement away from human experience. ✒ If you find yourself moving into the presence of God either by a very deep search in your own life or by the apparently accidental situations in which you find yourself, if you find yourself moving (to use an imaginative expression) toward the face of God, what you will see is the face of another human being. ✒ When you are most deeply in the presence of God, you will find yourself most deeply connected to other people. It's the paradox of the Incarnation that God really entered human experience. He literally became a human being. Became human. When you find yourselves in the presence of God, you will find yourselves always in the presence of other human beings. ✒ But more than that, you will not find yourself in the presence of other women and men at their best. What you will see when you see the face of God is the wounded face of other men and women, those things in us that are dark and frightened and that repel us from one another. ✒ When Abraham was in the presence of God, what was he bound up with? He was bound up with the sins of Sodom and Gomorrah, his almost hopeless search for people of justice. ✒ If you find yourself by choice or by something which has grown in you without a lot of your doing or a lot of your choosing, if you find yourself caught up into the mystery of Christ, you will find yourself drawn into what is wounded, and painful, and, finally, what is evil in other human beings. Abraham's goodness doesn't separate him from others; it makes him responsible for their evil. ✒ If you, in your life, are trying to live by the hope of the beatitudes, if you're trying to develop a simple heart, if you're trying to live more simply in a complex world, if you're trying to be compassionate and vulnerable and loving, if you're trying to move into the presence of the Father of Jesus, you will find yourself drawn into what is not simple and loving in other people. The very effort to live the Christian life will bind you to the rejection of the Christian life in other people. ✍ If you put on Christ, if you start to live in the mystery of Christ, you will be drawn into His death. He dies over and over again. The death of Jesus was not one simple moment in human history; it is the core of human history. God Himself plunged Himself into the harsh reality of human existence, became death, became sin, St. Paul says. It is not in escape from what's dark in ourselves, in other people, that we will find the love of God, but in letting ourselves be drawn into these things. It's a risky business. There's good sense in avoiding other people's faults, dark sides, and wounded parts and fears. ✍ If we're going to live with other people in a way in which we will be really alive to all the parts of human reality, the only passage is through the journey of prayer. I may find myself connected to what is least loving in other people, but I will find myself connected to it in the presence of God, only if I will pray for them, if I will enter the mystery, the emptiness of prayer. ✍ To be really connected to other people, to be

11

connected at the point about which we are talking here—at our weakness, at our failures—to be connected and not just repelled by them, not angry at them, not afraid of them, but really connected to them, we must come gradually into the whole story of human beings. ✒ What you will discover, finally, is that it is not just a story of failure, it's not just a story of anger, it's not just a story of fighting for who gets the best place, it's not just a story of fear, fear of our own weakness, fear of other people's demands. It is, finally, a story of love as the death of Jesus Christ was, finally, a story of love and not a story of death. The most crucial thing about a love story, about any love story, whatever form or shape it takes, is that, within the love story, the lovers discover themselves to be inevitably connected, inescapably bound together. ✒ Isn't that what people say? "We've got to stay together because we love one another." People separate when they discover they are no longer in love. Love is the thing that inescapably connects us whether we're connected by the flesh of a mother's womb, the common life of family or friends, the destiny of a nation. God is inescapably connected with us; and that's why the cross is a love story. ✒ Those things that are dark in us, that are wounded, that are evil, can destroy those connections. This is why we are driven back to prayer. This is why the search for God, although it takes place alone, is never lonely; because even the loneliest struggle to find God's will and to do it binds you to other people. ✒ If you are looking, however confidently or hesitantly, for the face of God, what you will see is a face that looks something like mine or the person's next to you. ✒ If you are looking for love, what you will find are not only the gifts, but the needs and failures of other people. If you are looking for life, you will be led through death. It's the drama of Jesus Christ that becomes present over and over again in the Eucharist, that's being lived out in each of your lives beyond this Eucharist.

In the Image of God

I'd like to say something about celebration. When we celebrate we use things (food and candles and music) to help us pay attention to something else. Celebration is a way of going underneath the facts of our life, which are always there, in order to touch the reality and power that underlie them. Somebody has lived a whole year, we celebrate her birthday: we pay attention to the *fact* that she's alive, and for the time of the birthday we pay attention to her in a way we don't usually pay attention so that we touch what is real and powerful underneath. ✦ A good analogy for this religious meaning of celebration is the role of creation in music and art. We 'create' music. The singer creates the song. While they are not identical, at every instant of the song there is the intimate presence of the singer. Take away the singer, the song disappears. Between anything and God, there is the relationship of song and Singer. The creature and God are not identical— the song is not the singer—but they are joined together with a kind of complete intimacy so that they are not separate. ✦

15

To say you are a creature is to say that
there is not any part of your being, not
any moment of your time, that is not intimately connected to God. There is nothing you can do to lose this presence of
God. There is nothing you can do to walk
away from it. It is the truth about you—
that at the very core of your being you are
God's creature. You are God's song. ✒
When I really pay attention to the things
around me, as I might when I pay attention to a work of art, I come into the
presence of the one who created it, into
the presence of her genius, of her power,
her sensitivity. So if I really allow myself
to be in the presence of the truth and
reality of anything, I will be in the presence of the Creator. I think what I've said
so far is not very difficult to understand.
Maybe we don't think that way much, but
at least it's close to something we
understand. ✒ The second part of celebration is a lot less easy to understand
because this is now not the celebration of
a thing which already exists. In this celebration a reality comes into being because
we're going to celebrate a Sacrament which
is not just a sign of what is already there

but is a sign, as the old catechism says, that produces what it signifies. ✒ We're going to celebrate a different kind of presence of God. We're going to celebrate something for which the best word is—a new creation. There will truly take place here a new creation. That is to say, a new way in which God is present. Not only is God the Being who creates the existence of this other, who holds her in existence, who makes every part of her an expression of His wisdom and power; but He's one who will become present—unlosably present in this human being in a way that's very hard to find words for. The Holy One will become present now, not through an act of power and love, but with His own life. ✒ It's as if there were something I could do which would connect me to you so intimately that we wouldn't be two anymore, but that actually at the heart of it we would be living the same life. The infinite Creator of the universe will become inescapably present in another human life in a radically new way, in a new creation. How do we find words to express this inner life of God? We can't name it because that would be to give it God's name, which we don't know. We can describe somewhat its own inner law. ✍

The inner dynamism of this life is the law of the Trinity. What was revealed most profoundly in the death and resurrection of Jesus—the Image of the unseen God— is this inner reality of God: the complete giving of the Self to the Other, and the complete acceptance of the Other as a gift of Self. Since God is, in fact, Reality in which everything else shares in order to be real, the Trinity is the inner law of all life. God's own being is this unimaginable total giving, receiving and sharing of the gift of self. ✍ In the world in which we live, in most of our experience, we experience ourselves as something to be protected from the other, as something to be guarded against the other, as something to rest in a certain amount of security that is ours. When we try to live by this inner law of the Trinity, by this inner presence of God to us in some special way, what we experience in our own life is that this gift of the self to the other and this willingness to accept the whole reality of the other is accomplished in pain, fear, threat. Indeed, what we meet is what Jesus met

when He lived by this inner law of Trinity.
✒ But our hope is that this experience
does not reveal the truth of things. We
believe that the deepest reality of things is
the gift of the self to the other and the
acceptance of the gift. Not just giving yourself away. It's giving and receiving *completely.* The only place we know of where
this happened is in the story of Jesus
Christ. And so in order to enter this new
creation, to become this new creature, this
infant will be baptized into the Body of
Christ. Only God could do that. ✒ In
this room we are not all Christians, but
we can all enter this celebration at some
important and truthful point. Pay attention to this baby girl—in music and candles
and silence. Celebrate, beneath the fact of
her existence, the mystery of her creature-
hood. In water and words, celebrate the
new presence of the mystery of Trinity,
this new creation of a member of the Body
of Christ.

In the Image of God

Being religious is a way of being human, one way among many possible ways. Being a believer is one way of being religious. It involves, among other things, the exploration of all the dimensions of human reality as possible places of meeting with God. How is my body possibly a place of meeting with God? or time, or choosing, or talents—or failure, or pain? What are the inner laws of such encounters? The role of the community is to make available to the believer the wisdom about these crucial questions that the tradition has accumulated. ✍
I'd like to talk for a while about one important dimension of human reality which plays a crucial role in the encounter with God on our various interior journeys: life as passion, drive, dynamism, movement. The believer explores the image of God in this dimension of human being by living her own reality in hope. ✍ Hope is one of those dynamic attitudes that allow the various movements of our life to be directed toward the person of God, the mysterious Holy One. Hope isn't a specific expectation. It's rather a kind of spirit

within the dynamic parts of our life. In the words of the old catechism, hope is one of the three virtues which make of our life a movement toward God. Because hope is this, because more than that, hope is a gift, something that God accomplishes in us, it isn't something that we can produce in ourselves. When we talk about being hopeful and living our life in hope, we're not talking ethics. We're not talking about some ideal that we should attempt to accomplish in ourselves. We're talking religion; that is to say, we're talking about something to be discovered and lived in response to God. ✒ Hope is something that is created within us. It's a way we are. It's a way we discover ourselves able to be. It is actually the presence of God drawing us toward Himself. So when we talk about being hopeful, when we have scripture readings (Wis 18:6–9; Heb 11:1–2, 8–19; Lk 12:32–48) calling us to be hopeful, the response is not that you have to go out and do something or try to do something. Hope isn't about anything specific. If it were about something specific, it wouldn't be hope and I think that's the point of the second reading today. If we're going to be hopeful, if we're gradually going to deepen in ourselves this way of living that we call hopefulness, what we have to do first of all is to be hopeful about ourselves. Just as, if we're going to be loving we have to be loving about ourselves first. Hopeful about ourselves. Hopeful about the people who are near us. 🖋 What would it mean for us to be hopeful about ourselves right now? That question, as all questions about Christian virtue, leads us to prayer. If we're going to answer that question we have to be present to ourselves in some prayerful and attentive ways. 🖋 If I am to be really hopeful about you, I have to pray about you. In that search for what it means for me to be really hopeful about you or about myself, as I pay enough attention, I will discover particular signs of what it is I am to be hopeful for. 🖋 But those things themselves are not the object of hope. They're the steps that we pass through. Just as Abraham had to keep passing through different moments: being called to a place, being moved to go to another, hoping to have a son, undergoing a test. All through his life there were these moments. And you move from one to the other because you find in yourself the ability to keep going and not to settle down. You find yourself with some great pain, with some great loss and you can settle in it and become hopeless. It's a real temptation: you can allow your life to be collapsed within the pain, within the loss. ✒ You find yourself with something very good going, and you can settle in it and become hopeless. Or, as Jesus said in the reading, "Your heart will be wrapped round where your treasure is." You can settle in it. Or you can continue to ask yourself in good times or in bad times, "What would it mean for me to be hopeful?" And in asking the question the next movement will eventually open itself up. ✒ Hope is that presence in our life which makes all the moments of our life converge toward where we finally belong: the heart of the divine Being. In all the movements of our life, there is a source of the true movement of our life, a source discovered only by hope, in hope. The most hopeful thing that you can say about yourself is, I guess, that you can be hopeful. If I asked you right now, "What do you think is hopeful about me?" you

might not be able to answer because we
don't think about things that way. We
don't think about ourselves that way. What
all three of these readings are saying is
that we've got the gift to be hopeful about
ourselves and hopeful about one another.
That is to say, we have the gift, which is
most deeply expressed in prayer, to discover in the passions and dreams and drives
of our life the real journey of our selves
back to the mystery of God.

In the Image of God

In some ways these read-
ings (Jer 38: 4–6, 8–10;
Heb 12: 1–4; Lk 12: 49–53)
are a continuation of the readings about the reality of hope.
What hope means in human experience.
How hopefulness organizes the dynamics
of human life toward an encounter with
God. I'll come back to that in a moment,
but let's begin in the way the scriptures
begin today, with a series of images of
people in the presence of God. Right now
just try to think of a really good image of
a human being in the presence of God.
I strongly suspect that nobody here
has come up with a picture of somebody
drowning in mud. That's the first image
in the scriptures today. The prophet in
the presence of God was being enveloped
in mud at the bottom of a well!
There is a second image of a human being
completely absorbed by God—his whole
life moving toward God. Now not the
tragic and comic figure of a man dumped
into a well, but the image of death, of a
man dying on the cross, a man of trouble
around whom things divide in half, where

27

people slip and fail, a man in a maelstrom.
⚜ I imagine that most of our images of
people absorbed in the presence of God
are images of peace and serenity. Think of
most religious statues. But here we have
these two pictures. When your life is all
coordinated toward the mysterious presence of God, this is what you look like:
one man suffocating in mud at the bottom of a well, the other dying a failure.
And both of them are images of hope,
precisely because the images are dominated
by evil and trouble. ⚜ The presence of
evil and your response to the presence of
evil have everything to do with how you
encounter God in your own life. Entering
into the presence of God is not accomplished by fleeing from your own evil or
trouble or other people's evil or trouble.
The image of being with God as somehow being calm, peaceful, untroubled,
unburdened by things is a false image. It's
a dangerously false image because it makes
us neglect that quality of our own experience, or those places in our own experience, which really are the places of meeting with God. ⚜ Over and over again

in Christian religious experience there have

been stories, sayings and warnings not to settle for false gods. It's the particular temptation of religious people—that is, of people who find themselves, by their own choice or by something in their lives, caught up with this mysterious presence of God. There is a quality in their lives that connects them to this whole question of God and the reality of God. People who are so constituted, who lead such lives, must seek the wisdom that allows them not to make mistakes about the real God and false gods—about the real presence of God and the illusions. ⚘ And one of the places where we're most likely to make mistakes has to do with trouble. Trouble and evil. God is met only when we don't run away from the evil that's in ourselves and in other people. When we don't run away from it from discouragement, weariness or out of fear. Over and over again you find it in yourself or hear it said, "Good Lord, to try to find justice in the world is incredibly difficult. How can we accomplish anything against the massiveness of evil? There's nothing you can do about it." ⚘ I'm sure there are similar things in your own life, things in yourself that discourage you because they seem to have been there endlessly. So you say the best thing to do is forget about it. ✒ Jeremiah suffocating upside down in the mud. (I don't know why I think of him as upside down in the mud.) Jeremiah was thrown in there by hostility. It was because Jeremiah was facing, was living this— I'm deliberately trying to choose these verbs because when we get to the point of saying, "OK, we've really got to deal with evil," we deal with it in an evil way. We think that the only way to confront evil is with anger or the only way to confront evil is by attacking it or destroying it. That's not true. First of all, you have to recognize in yourself all of those places which are possibly places of meeting with God. Ask yourself, "What is the image of a human being in the presence of God?" What kind of image do you have? Usually it is an image of everything going all right—when there's a good deal of affection. I'm not saying these things are not signs of the presence of God. The trouble is they're only half the sign. ✒ We come back to hope. As we said last time, hope is precisely that kind of dynamism in ourselves that lets our life organize itself to move toward God. It's not something that we do. You can't make yourself hopeful. It's not an ethical accomplishment. It is a creation of God in you. To reach your own hopefulness, you've got to reach that point in yourself where God is creating hope in you. Because that's what it is. It is what God creates in us that moves us toward Him. So hope is not about anything. If I said to you, "Let's all be hopeful!" it would be a mistake to ask, "Well, what will we hope for?" Hope isn't about something. You can be hopeful about sad things and hopeful about happy things. Hope is not an emotion. It's the whole way in which you are in the world. ✒ So, you have to be hopeful about particular things, but your hope has to move you past them. I think it's really well said in the first prayer: "May we love you in all things, but above all things." Really loving the things but not settling down in them. That's the trick of Christianity. Not to love God by leaving things and not to pretend that the things are gods—but to love the things, to love the people, really to love them, to be bound up with them, be bound with them as they are, as you are, with all the trouble, with all the evil. 🖋 If you really are going to meet God where he is to be found, the meeting will take place where good and evil meet and confront one another. If you're going to meet God, you have to meet him on His terms. That is to say that you meet Him there the way Christ did. The struggle between good and evil is the struggle where finally the evil can be overcome and transformed by the good. You don't have to answer evil with evil. You don't have to answer other people's discouragement with your own. You don't have to answer other people's anger with your own. You don't have to answer your own sin with self-hatred. That's the endless confrontation of evil with evil. But if you're really in the presence of evil and yet you live that conflict between good and evil as Jesus did, if the real point of conflict in your life is the place where you meet God, then it's going to have the characteristics of God. It is going to be full of life and hopeful, and finally it's going to have the features of God's own being, as St. John tells us.

As I've said often before, our sacred books are meant, aside from what they reveal about the inner life of the Holy One, to uncover for us the structures and possibilities of human life and the world as places for the journey of Faith. They are sacred books because they point to those dimensions of human experience which can become places of encounter with God. They also express the inner structure of that kind of experience: what it is like to be in God's presence in this or that dimension of our life. Sacred books have to do with the nature and the possibilities of religious experience. And that's especially true of the scriptural selections that we read between the end of the Easter cycle and the beginning of Advent. ⚹ Last week, the readings dealt with *things*, to show how something that can be possessed and consumed can become a place of encounter with God. How things can be a place of meeting with God. And it was a marvelous story. The story of the rich man and Lazarus. The rich man lives very well, does very well. Outside his house lives this impover-

33

ished man. They both die. One goes to heaven. One goes to hell. The rich man in hell and...and the rest of the story. That's a story not about good guys and bad guys and people getting it in the end because they had it too good while they were here. It's a story about the possibility of religious experience in things. ✣ And the key to that story, I think, is the character of the rich man, and the key to the character of the rich man is his generosity. He's an extraordinarily generous and other-directed person. He's probably one of the least selfish of the characters who appear in the whole of the New Testament. And the reason I say that is the way he behaves when he's in hell. You remember he asks to be helped and Abraham says, "You can't be helped. There's a gulf between us and you. You've crossed some sort of divide in being. You are among those who don't love and we are among those who have discovered love." How does the rich man react? "Well, send somebody to help my brothers because they're living the way I did. I have five brothers, better they shouldn't end up like me." An extraordinary, generous man. ✣ How many people here in anything like an equivalent predicament would react like that? Where we find ourselves in the slightest uncomfortable position, stuck on an expressway, trapped by exams, for how many of us is our first reaction, "I hope nobody else has to suffer this." Not very many! ✒ The point about Dives is that he is mistaken about whom his life is connected to. Once he has a sense of whom he is connected to, he knows what life is about. He knows it's about sharing reality, but he doesn't understand whom he's connected to. He thinks only that he's connected to his brothers. He never understands. If he had ever noticed the poor man outside his house, a man of that kind of generosity would obviously have shared things with him. But he never notices him. He never realizes how the things that he could own or possess are actually the presence of things to be shared with other people, and so he ends up missing the point of his own life and missing God in his life. ✒ An apparently simple question is actually a very daring one, if we ask it seriously and follow out its implications: who am I, and to whom is my life connected? Lived thoroughly and attentively, it is, in fact, the key question which opens up the life of faith. How do you answer that question? "I'm an engineering student, that's who I am. I'm an engineering student preparing for a career in this place and I live in this country and I have to get a certain kind of job and because of that I'm connected to certain kinds of people who can help me, and other people are none of my business. I'm connected to certain people who can help—and other people, they're just not there." "I'm so-and-so's daughter, or so-and-so's mother, or so-and-so's son and so-and-so's husband or so-and-so's wife, that's who I am, and because of that I'm connected de da de da de da." ✍ How do you answer that question? Who are you? And being who you are, to whom is your life really connected? Although it may not seem to be so at first, it is a question about whether or not you meet the sacred in your life. ✍ Today's reading (Lk 17: 5–10) takes up from there in order to explore further the place of 'things' in the journeys of faith. At first sight, it's an extraordinarily shocking reading. The image of God that

Jesus presents here is almost revolting. The image of a self-centered master who has no sense of gratitude for what's done for him. "You did what you were supposed to do, what do you want? Just go and wait on me further!" ✒ The part of our life that is our own construction, the part of our life that is a response to the sense of duty, doing what we're supposed to do, is an expression of our own freedom; it is an expression of us. If what you have made of your own life is all right, is pretty good, is that a place where you meet God? Amazingly he says, "No, it is not." Allow yourself to be driven as far as this shocking statement goes, because if you go far enough in it, it will turn your thinking upside down and you will see what He's really talking about. Jesus is not given to blasphemous and ugly presentations of God—but shocking ones, yes. Shocking in order to tumble us out of our ordinary way of experiencing ourselves in the world. ✒ You look at your own life. You have lived that life with an attempt to do the right thing, to do what you have the gifts to do. Are you now in the presence of God? No. Because the crucial thing to

learn is that the encounter with God cannot be something of your own making.
The meeting between you and God cannot be a product of your own freedom, of
your own choices, no matter how good
they are. The meeting between you and
God is a meeting of *two* freedoms: His
and yours, His and mine. The world that
I've made, the decent things I've done,
the right things or indeed the wrong
things, are always only a possible place of
meeting. ✒ Just as in another shocking
aside, the Gospel seems to say that it
doesn't even matter very much whether
your own world is a good one or a failure.
The second kind, in fact, was more often
a place of meeting God than the first. You
might be making a really decent and good
human world. On its own terms, it cannot
be the place of encounter. ✒ You're
going to meet God at that point where
His freedom breaks into the world you've
made. Go back to the question I asked,
whether you've thought about it before
or not. Something will come to mind. Who
are you connected to in your life? What is
there between you and them right now?
Where is there the possibility of something

radically new? Of something that would be a new exchange of hope or service or love? The world that I have constructed, that I am able to live in is not the world where I meet God. I will meet the Holy One at that place where His creative freedom is unexpectedly breaking into that world I've made. There is in my life and in yours now, a place where there is a possibility for a radical exchange of new life, of hoping, of love, of challenge, of forgiveness. ✒ This is such a crucial thing for Christ that he uses this bizarre story. When you have done all that you are supposed to do, just say to yourself, "I'm a useless servant." But servant is not the name of the relationship between us and God. It is friend. The first thing they said to Him was, "Increase our faith," and His answer was very interesting. He said, "You don't need more faith, you need to notice where the faith is already. You need to notice where the miracles are already happening." ✒ Who are you? Who am I? To whom does that link me? And in those links, where is this extraordinary and unexpected and terrifying exchange of gifts taking place? If you want to meet the Holy One whom Jesus knew, you have to meet Him at the point where death meets resurrection.

Most often when we hear these passages from Scripture (Is 66: 18–21; Heb 12: 5–7, 11–13; Lk 13: 22–30) we find ourselves discouraged and frightened. They are, indeed, readings of profound challenge—but not to some moral reform which is beyond human achieving. These readings are part of a whole series of readings about what it's like to be in the presence of God, about the Kingdom of God, or more accurately, God's rule, God's presence in the time and space of human experience. And that *is* a thing to be afraid of because that really is a tough test. ✣ Living in the world with hope, which is one part of living as a believer, has little or nothing to do with feeling reassured or with having an optimistic temperament. Faith does not trivialize the experience of being human; indeed, as you can see in the lives of great believers, it deepens it and radicalizes it. We all know that being a human being is a great task, and one in which failure is a real possibility. It is possible to come to the end of our life and say, "It wasn't worth being me." ✣ If religious faith were to claim that the enormous challenge of being human could be met in some simple-minded and easily achievable formulas, it would have no right to claim the attention of real women and men. If I said to you, "Oh, you can have a perfect marriage. There are only two things you have to do, and they each take 36 seconds," you would say, "Ridiculous! He doesn't have any idea how deep and complicated being married really is." Then why should we think that living—not in the presence of another human being—but in the presence of Infinite Knowledge and Infinite Love should be something easily grasped and quickly done? ✒ Being hopeful is a way of living human life at its mysterious depths, with a constant awareness of its challenge and possible tragedy. These readings about the many called and few chosen, about the narrow door through which we must enter the presence of God, are readings about hope. ✒ They are not, I think, warnings about doing bad things, which is the way most of us first hear them. Everybody remembers her own private obsessions: "Here I am, still doing the same things, still failing in the same old ways." But notice the text. The people who are excluded are not people who are not trying, people simply wallowing in their own private vices. It's talking about people who are trying to be in the presence of God, who are trying to live their life at its real depth. And it's saying that this is not an easy thing to do.

✤ The challenge of living in hope does not escape any of the challenges which are the very stuff of the human adventure, but it includes them in another challenge which cuts to the very heart of the task of being a human freedom in the world. If we are going to live in God's presence, then we're going to live in God's presence and not our own. A tautology that hides an adventure of astounding and constant challenge and surprise. The temptation against hope is the temptation to live in a world constructed by ourselves, and not in the real world, which is being created by God. ✤ Many people who try to enter the presence of God enter it without any room for the unexpected. They're sure of what should follow. They know what comes next. They know how to behave—and in doing that, they exclude the possibility of

43

an encounter with God. ✒ We enter God's presence not by always doing the right thing in the best way, but by struggling with the evil we find in ourselves and outside ourselves. There is a mistaken fear of our own evil which drives us away from the presence of God into the false peace of our own idols and illusions.

We said last time that it is not an easy or simple thing to be a human being or a believer. But we should be sure to grasp the difficulty and challenge of this life in the right way and for the right reasons. Many times we make human life difficult, almost impossible, but for all the wrong reasons. Religious people frequently imagine the life of faith in ways that are not only profoundly difficult and depressing, but also completely wrong-headed. ✍ While profound, and subtle and richly complex, being a believer has an inner simplicity. In order to think about it, however, we have to examine it from many angles, see it in its different aspects and moments, and use a language which has all the awkwardness of something coming from other experiences. If we are really to live as believers, more and more humanly and freely, we have to use our thinking and language, and then break beyond them to the life of faith. ✍ The religious use of ordinary language and stories is often meant to invite us to think, sometimes to break up our ordinary way of thinking, and so to send us back to the

experience of human life ready for the unexpected, attentive to possibilities present
in our experience but usually unnoticed.
We learn how to live in hope and so discover the possibilities of our world as a
place of encounter with God. Jesus called
this "the Kingdom of God."   ✍   The
readings today (1 Kgs 19 and Lk 14: 7–14)
are all about "hope" as one of the inner
laws of the life of a believer. The first reading gives the key to all the rest and sets
the framework for thinking about the others as linked. The first reading says straight-
forwardly: You have come into the very
presence of God. It goes through all the
classical symbols of theophanies: fire,
storm, wind, earthquake—but God is in
none of these. And then, the almost unnoticed sound. Why does the prophet know
at that moment that God is there?   ✍   In
this presence of God—so strangely revealed
to a man defeated in his struggle for justice and so depressed he wants to die—we
are asked by the Church to listen to these
two stories. I couldn't figure out why the
two of them were together. They don't
appear to go together. The first one seems
to be one of those stories of good com-

mon sense. Don't stick your head out too far. If you want to get ahead in the world, read the world you're in very carefully, and calculate what you can do to be the biggest success. Like Uriah Heap, "Be 'umble Urie, be 'umble, and you'll get ahead." Take the lowest place and good things will happen to you. That's what the story seems to be about. All right, you say, I can understand that, and, indeed, you can even say the same thing in less pejorative ways; such as, "Don't have such exalted a view of yourself; don't be foolishly vain." You can say it in ways that don't sound meretricious and self-serving. ✍ But then, what can you do when you get to the second story? The second story says when you give a party you should not invite any of your friends. Don't invite your relatives, don't invite anybody who can conceivably love you back, but invite all the people who can't. Now the one thing you can say immediately is that that is not good sense. It's probably not even healthy psychology. Anybody who lived by this image of his life would be a very destructive personality. ✍ So I'm saying to myself, "Why are these two stories

47

together?" The second is one of those ex-
treme stories that tumble us over into another world. And yet, the more you keep
thinking about the first story, the more
you will begin to see it growing toward
the second story. They are not just super-
ficially connected because they're both stories about people at parties. There is a
deeper connection. Is the first story really
good common sense? Does it really say
that you should calculate your world well
and live in it so that you will not go beyond the bounds of your life-situation, and
so succeed?   ✍   Or, when you really
allow the characters of the story to become more and more vivid to you, do you
realize that the story is about *not* control-
ling your environment at all? The story really says you don't know who is invited to
this party. You're living in a world that
you do not control. You could take the
lowest place and then, in fact, be the lowest one! You would have chosen correctly,
for you might find that everybody who
has been invited is more noble than you
are. It doesn't say that in always taking
the lowest place you will always be the
best person there. It just says that you are

living in a world in which you have to risk something other than your own calculations. And that begins to move us toward the second story. ✒ If you take these out of the figurative form that they're in and put them into some kind of abstract form, I think it would be something like, "Live your life, deal with other people as if (this is not the right way but I'm going to say it just to get it out of my mind) radically you do not matter." But I don't want to say that because it's too banal and I don't think that's really what it's saying. ✒ I will give you the image I have in my mind, and maybe you can make some sense of it. You come to the Eucharist and you are told that you are in the presence of God, and what you're given is a piece of bread, and sometimes for you it is nothing but a piece of bread. Now, you meet other people and very often they are nothing but other people because you meet them with all your calculations about what they mean. The one who invites the poor and the crippled is inviting the unexpected. ✒ What's the difference between having a party to which you invite the poor, the crippled and the lame and going to communion and being given a piece of bread? If the Eucharist, being handed a piece of bread, is a meeting with God, that can only be because in living with other people there is the possibility of such an encounter.   *ɰ*   St. Paul says we can receive the Eucharist to our own destruction, because we do not discern the presence of God—for us, it's just bread. If we live in our world without the hopefulness that allows us to respond to the unexpected presence of God, we can live our lives to our own destruction. During the silence, consider the people you are now living with—but think of them with hope, with a readiness for the unexpected. How much do we calculate about the people whom we meet? And in doing so, do we exclude what is really there but which can be met only when we approach others with the paradoxical attitude by which we take a piece of bread in our hand and know that it is God? What would the people in our world be like lived with in this way?

Today is the Feast of the Body of Christ, the Feast of Corpus Christi, the Feast of the Eucharist, the Feast of the presence of God in the world. In the first reading from Genesis (Gn14: 18–20), we have the mysterious story of Abraham's meeting with the priest Melchizedek. Abraham has just had a great triumph over people who were trying to destroy him; he's on his way back with a lot of spoils. He meets Melchizedek. The warrior, obviously soiled by hand-to-hand combat, meets this hieratic and strange figure who comes from nowhere and goes away again after this one incident, who offers a sacrifice not of blood, but of bread and wine, a sacrifice of life. That's one story. ⚜ The other story (1 Cor 11: 23–26) is a story within a story about a group of Christians getting together at the Eucharist and reading or having read to them the story of what Jesus did on the night before He died. And the last (Lk 9: 11–17), the familiar story about the multiplication of the loaves, the great crowds, religious enthusiasm, healing, human hunger and this extraordinary abundance of

51

food and life coming out of want. ✧
All three of them, all three of the images,
all three of the stories are stories about a
meeting between the Holy One and human beings, between God and man, just
as the Eucharist is about the meeting between God and human beings. There are
just two fairly short things I'd like to say
today of the many things the Eucharist
means and suggests. ✧ Whenever we
think about God, whenever the idea of
God comes to us or some information
about God, the root human experience is
that of the enormous distance between us
and God. The root human experience is
not one of encounter, but of absence. The
distance between myself and God is, first
of all, a kind of metaphysical distance, a
distance between my reality and the divine reality. There is a gulf of being between myself and the Holy One. ✧
There is another distance between me and
God which is the result not of just exist-
ing as a creature, but of fault. The distance that is partly willed and partly, it
seems, fate. The distance of our own un-
lovingness, turning in on ourselves, fear,
arrogance, all of those things that separate

us from the life of the Holy One either by our own choice or by the way we find ourselves to be, by the way we have been shaped by others. ⚜ The first thing the Eucharist says to us is that there is an encounter between God and us which can take place between the priest and the man just back from killing: it can take place in the midst of a crowd which at any moment could turn ugly or violent, suddenly aware only of its need to eat. It can take place in the quiet of a last meal among friends or in a group of people who are meeting and remembering. ⚜ There is an encounter between us and God. There is a presence of the Holy in my life and it's rooted in His love for me. A love that does not respond to what is good, but which creates. A love that loves what is for me unlovable, what is in fact unlovable. I don't really know what more to say about that because I think from that point on it becomes not private but radically personal. In some particular ways I think what is unlovable for us is the most special thing. It is where we are most ourselves and the place where we least expect to be found. ⚜ This brings me to the

53

second thing I want to say. It is very significant that the story about the multiplication of the loaves and fish has always
been linked in the minds of Christians with
the presence of God in the world; not as a
source of magical escape from trouble and
not because you can find what you need
without any work, but because they realize (and in this translation it's particularly good) that, first of all, the miracle
takes place in a lonely place. ✒ They
are in a lonely place and the heart of the
story is in the one sentence where He says,
"You feed them." In other words, Christians have realized that the crucial thing
about the meeting with God is accepting
the challenge that we are food for one another. They set out to feed them with
what they've got. They don't go to buy
anything else; they don't cut the people
off. They just say, "O.k., in what I am, I
am food for others." In their gesture God
becomes present in that place. He becomes
present as food (which is one of the ways
He becomes present), but the crucial part
of the story is that God becomes present
in that place. ✒ And the people who
come back the next day and say, "Listen,

we want more food," are the ones who have missed the point. When I think about myself and God, I am confronted, as any human being is confronted, with the temptation of the distance between us: the radical distance which is the distance in being; the truthful distance, which is the distance of my own life story, what has been laid upon me by others and what I have laid upon myself. What the Eucharist says is that beneath all that, within all that, God can be present. ✒ The next thing concerns the consequences in our lives of the truth of this presence of God. Where would we be led in our lives if consistently and seriously, despite all the inevitable failures and compromises, we were to say each day, "You are food for me. Your very being is my food, and I am food for you"? Where would we be led by this? I think in Stony Brook, more vividly than in many other places on Long Island, we're aware that we're in a lonely place. ✒ If we reaffirm our loneliness we will never meet God. For people like us who live in the middle of a radically secularized culture, a suburban culture, a culture that has lost all symbols of connection to say that we are food for one another is really bizarre. That's why what we're faced with is a crisis of faith, not a moral crisis. It's a question of whether or not we believe that God is really present in the way He is present. We have nothing to feed one another we say, because it's lonely here. You are food for one another He says.

All through Advent there is an accent on a dimension of Christian experience which is crucial, but subtle and dangerous. Crucial, because without it there is a serious distortion of the Christian life. Dangerous because it's the dimension of that experience which, itself, can be very easily distorted and which has to be lived with great prudence. We're talking about that dimension of Christian experience which is the experience of the absence of God, what is referred to in more dynamic terms during Advent as the experience of longing or expectation. ✒ I mentioned last week that there is a part of this experience which has to do with an experience of personal isolation and loneliness. While we have to talk about that at some point, I think it's dangerous, especially for us who are so marked by psychological metaphors and for whom there is always a tendency to over-psychologize rather than to understand things religiously. There are, anyway, other aspects of this experience which play important roles in the life of faith. ✒ The experience of the absence of God is a way of experiencing the world. It's a way of experiencing what is not God. We always meet God in what is not God, we never meet God directly. So, to talk about experiencing the absence of God is to talk about a way of being in the world. To talk about experiencing the absence of God is to talk about the way you experience different dimensions of the reality and the people that are around you. Last week we talked about two of them. The first includes all those things which are collected under the notion of violence: not only physical violence, direct physical violence, but everything that violence evokes, everything that is involved in the conjunction of victims and victimizers. And that is everywhere. It is in the way people are together in the dorms, it's in the scholastic world, it's in business, it's in the neighborhoods around here—it's within your own interpersonal relationships. Everybody knows that. ✒️ How would we live in such a world *without* experiencing the absence of God? That's the way we do try to live most of the time. We create a world in which we are untouched by the reality of violence around us. This can be either a physical world which we construct, a place safe and quiet, the very epitome, I suppose, of what we mean by "bourgeois"; or it can be an interior world. It can be a world in which we're simply unaffected, apathetic, in which our feelings are untouched by the reality of the victims and the victimizers who are around us. ✍ To withdraw into such a world is to say in effect, "The violence is the way things are. That's the way things are in business; that's the way things work here at Stony Brook. That's what you've got to do to make it. That's just the way things are." Do you see how this is *not* to experience the violence as the absence of God? To say, rather, that such violence is not the reality of things, that what is at the heart of life is the possibility of the transformation of the victimizers and the victims: this is to experience these evils as the absence of God. ✍ The second dimension of the absence of God which I mentioned last week has to do with the way we experience one another—to use the advent word for it—with expectation, think about one another with expectation. Think about the people you live with. The people who may be part of your family or

the people you work with or the people in
the hall or the people in your classes. What
would it mean to think about them with
expectation? To experience them with
expectation? ✒ The heart of this dimension of Christian experience is prayer—
praying for one another. I suggested last
week that the content of this prayer largely
consists in learning to ask the right questions about one another. Think of the
people you live with, think of the people
you work with—that whole list that I just
went through. What are the right questions for you to be asking about this one
or that one? What are the right questions
that you should be asking about me, and
I about you? That's a very important part
of our praying for one another. It is the
very core of our praying for one another.
If I really experienced you, thought about
you with expectation, what questions
would I be trying to raise about you in
praying? In meeting you, do I experience
the absence of God, or do I just take you
for what you are and there it is and that's
the end of it? ✒ A third dimension of
this complex but important experience of
the absence of God is touched on today

and especially in the figure of John the
Baptist. It is repentance—the experience
of repentance. To grasp this most fully,
the best thing to do would be to get really vividly and imaginatively involved with
this man John the Baptist, but that must
be done in meditation, not in the brief
time of a homily.   If you want to
know what a human being looks like who
is living in a state of permanent repentance, who is really in touch with this dimension of human life, she or he would
look like John the Baptist. A human being
living in repentance would look like this
"mad" figure, John the Baptist, clothed in
animal skins, eating what he finds here
and there. What is evoked by that? Now
that's where the imagination can really go
on but I'm going to slip immediately into
a kind of descriptive abstraction.   This
suggests for us that to live in repentance is
to be in touch with a profound possibility
of freedom in yourself. It's to seek in yourself this capacity for a kind of radical lib-
eration and freedom. If I say to you that
it's possible for you to repent, or that you
ought to repent, what I'm talking about is
that your life is not a simple summation of

all the things that have happened up to
now; that you're not now just a collection
of inevitabilities; that you're not trapped
within whatever limitations have been built
into you by the choices you've made, by
the things that have happened to you. ✒
If you are inevitably what you are, you
can't repent. To talk about repentance is
to say that there is the possibility for return toward a radical freedom which can
carry beyond what is failed and limited.
Take very simple examples of it. Perhaps
out of fear or lust or something like that,
you have built certain necessities into your
life. "This is the way I am." "This is the
way I do it." "This is what I need." And
some of these things are vicious. To say to
yourself it is possible to repent, is to say
that it's possible for you to escape those
limitations. ✒ To accept the possibility
of repentance is to take up the challenge
of living the depths of human experience—
of living as a believer. It is to acknowledge
in yourself a capacity to love, and a capacity to know which connect you with reality, through very simple and particular
things. To love this person. To know this
truth. To have this job. To possess this

thing. Yet to live all of this ordinary human experience with repentance is to experience in all these things the absence of
God. 🖋 While we live with all these
things, while they answer our inner drives,
we cannot rest in them. We cannot say,
"Now this is enough. Now I am at home.
This is where I belong." To live in repentance is a scary thing to do. To live in a
real world, not to retreat into some other
world of imagination—to live in this real
world where you have to love this person
or know that thing., where you need this
or that to live and yet to say to yourself
that's not God. That's not the final word.
That's not the last story. There's a further
freedom possible. 🖋 When I say that
when you live in the world of repentance,
when you experience the possibility of repentance, the absence of God in things
and people around you, that you're nowhere, I don't mean that it's just a world
of chaos and anarchy. You are always seek-
ing to distinguish between illusion and
reality. Every step I take, every choice I
make, every time I open my mouth, every
person I'm with and every way I'm with
every person involves me in some kind of

judgment about what is illusion and what is reality. The violence in the world—is that illusion or reality? We come back to that extraordinary first reading (Is 11: 1–10) in which the prophet pushes everything together. He speaks of all of the dichotomies we live with: the dichotomies of the lion and the lamb, and everything else that goes with that. All of those dichotomies are illusion. The reality, he says, is a profound communion that is growing between everything that is real. In the world of violence that you and I live in inevitably, what is illusion and what is reality—violence or forgiveness? In the world you live in, what is illusion—the sins that have built you into where you are or the freedom that is offered by repentance? Which is reality? The God who is not yet here or the world as it is now? Which is the illusion and which is the reality?

This is the night on which we celebrate the birth of Jesus Christ, and meditate on the mysterious truth of the "Enfleshing" of God. To do this humanly and truthfully, we need to become more and more simple. God became a human being. That's all there really is to say about a night like this. It doesn't need embellishment. It just needs attentiveness, readiness for the unexpected. Since God is always the unexpected, we must learn how to live in readiness for it. To be simple enough and free enough to recognize and respond to the unexpected.

The great obstacle to this lies in the fact that there is something deeply wrong and troubled about that which is most human in us: our ability to know and our capacity to be present to another's reality, that is, our capacity to love *fail* where they ought not to. There's a woundedness about being human. We're all aware of this wound within the story of our own life or between us and other people. We meet it everywhere in the human story. It's the very stuff of our political experience, that there is something deeply wounded and troubled in us. It's the very human dimension of the extraordinary events of our own civilization—the intellectual and technological explosions that are the reality of the life which we live. The human dimension of these things remains full of questions, troubles and challenges. You don't live in a place like Stony Brook without knowing, besides the splendor of being human and its extraordinary force and creativity, that there is also something troubled in us. Anybody who has tried to love or let herself be loved knows that there are wounded things in us as human beings. And anybody who's created another human life knows this, too. It is to this troubled depth in ourselves that the simple statement is made: "God became a human being." ✒ Among many other things, one thing of which the Incarnation speaks is God's poverty. It is a *good* thing to be human as we are, with all the woundedness. And it is possible to enter, with all the freedom you're capable of, with all the intelligence and passion you're capable of, into the wounded and troubled parts of your own life or of the lives of other people. It is

possible to enter and live there *lovingly*.
🖋 This is what the readings (Is 52: 7–10,
Heb 1: 1–6, Jn 1: 1–18) are saying. If I'm
going to hear the truth of the Incarnation
I'm going to hear it in that place in myself
where the poverty of God expresses itself,
where Divine Being chooses to be intimate
to my being. In the places in myself that
are dark and wounded, the places that I
fear in myself and in other people, the
places that seem *not* to be places of life.
This is the extraordinary news of the Incarnation: even that in us which is sin can
be a place of meeting with God.   🖋
God became a human being. The truth
that is expressed inadequately by the word
"Incarnating," the "Incarnation" of God,
is the reality that we try to hold at the
center of our awareness during this time,
especially during the time of Mass or
prayer.   🖋 During this season of the
year we live, even if only at the edge of
our consciousness, with the awareness of
the truth that God became a real human
being. The fact in itself is so extraordinary—so obviously at the limits of
our capacity to grasp—and yet it has been
spoken of so often during the last two

thousand years that it has become for us a commonplace. ✒ In both directions we find an adequate response difficult: a truth that overwhelms us; a statement which has been trivialized and sentimentalized throughout the years. That is why art plays such an important role in reflecting on the Incarnation; music, and painting and literature, things which can break open our sensitivities. I am not an artist. I don't have any art at my command right now, so I'm simply going to say it again. ✒ It is true that He was a real human being, and the "He" in this case is God. The Divine Omnipotent Creator of the universe really became a man. The Scriptures read at the Christmas Mass insist on the reality of this. He not only became a man, an individual over there, off there by himself, a theophany of the divine, but He entered into the very texture of human relations. ✒ To be human means to be involved in this intimate network of responsibilities and possibilities and gifts. And that's what's insisted upon by this feast of the family. He didn't become "a man," an isolated moment of peak experience. He became human in the most complete and utter and banal and oppressive and good senses of that word. He was tied to other people, to their needs and to their faults, to their limits, to His own limits. ✍ He was caught up in that which is both the splendor and the oppression of human life—responsibility. He was responsible for them. Anyone who has had a child knows the extent of the burden and of the gift of responsibility. Anyone who has seen the person who gave you life grow old and become like a child—needy and dependent—knows the weight of human responsibility. This texture of human reality, God entered. ✍ I have said the facts— the truth that's revealed here. That He who was the divine Son of the divine Father became a human being and lived a human life with all of its network of experiences. How extraordinary a thing one human life is that it could actually bear the weight of a divine Person. That the network, that the texture of responsibility that I find myself bound by, called to, limited by, pressed upon by and opened up by—that network of responsibility was capable of expressing the very person of God. It could become the flesh of God.

And I mean again not just the peak experiences of my life but all the most banal parts of it too, all of the saddest parts as well as the great, expansive parts. 🖊

The Incarnation not only uncovers the depth of what it is to be human, but it also expresses in a way most available to us what God is like. What an act of love is present in that human life—is expressed in that human life! For God to become human and to live a human life. There is no explanation for it but love. What an awareness you can have of yourself as loved by Him. There's that terrific line in St. Paul's letter to the Romans, "After such a gift could He refuse anything He could give?" To *know* yourself to be surrounded by that kind of love! 🖊 One last remark. The Incarnation is a fact and a truth. It's at the limits of facts and truths, so it's hard to speak of, hard to hold yourself even for an instant in its full presence. You pile up all the words or you use the music or the art or the literature to bring this to consciousness and you know you're going to be there just for an instant of recognition. The implications of that instant of recognition have to do with human life itself, its capacity to be God's life, and also have to do with this insight into the very inner nature of God. His utterly reliable love for us. ✍ You could get this far and still have the sense that it's some kind of *other* reality—to be thought about, contemplated, responded to, touched occasionally. But it's not just that. The Incarnation is the very *law* of being. It is, if you get to the very heart of being, of any being, of anything that is real and especially of human being. The law of living like a human being is expressed in the reality of the Incarnation. How can you be in the presence of this extraordinary creative love? By following the law of the Incarnation. By following the very network of your own, the reality of your own human being into its depths. How did God transform the world? Overcome evil? Create new possibilities? By an exercise of infinite creative power? A sort of burst of new being? No. He did it by becoming a human being. That's all. The inner law of the transformation of the universe is the Incarnation.

In the Image of God

What do we mean when we say of a reading, "This is the word of God"? Have you ever wondered about that? One of the things we mean is that this statement or story can uncover for us something of the inner reality of God and at the same time—and necessarily—something of our own inner reality. Since whatever in us is real shares in the reality of God, we can't uncover any truth about God without at the same time grasping the truth of ourselves in a new way. 𝄢 Today's feast of Mary, the Mother of God, focuses our attention on the reality of the Godhead in the man Jesus. The revelation that Mary is really the mother of God, not just the mother of a man, expresses something of peculiar importance about the way God entered human history in the Incarnation. The Incarnation is also one of the inner laws of our own encounter with God, and this feast expresses something of peculiar importance about the way God continues to enter human life. 𝄢 This plunging into history by the Godhead, this immersing of Himself in the textures and structures, the relationships and responsibilities of human life, indeed, (if it's not too extravagant to talk this way) this passion of God to be with human beings was not accomplished by a one-sided exercise of infinite power. God became man through an encounter with human freedom. Thinking about this is crucial for our hearing the story of the Incarnation as "the Word of God." ✍

Probably as challenging as anything that could be said about the Incarnation is the statement that God's entrance into human history comes by way of the mutual agreement between Him and one human being. God's free choice—because the Incarnation is on God's part an act of freedom, not of some necessary overflowing of the Divinity—God's free choice needs to be answered by human freedom. Mary is not only the instrument of the Incarnation, she is a partner in it. ✍ This truth suggests two important aspects of our own freedom. First of all, we can realize in the light of the Incarnation that we experience our own freedom at its deepest truth as a response. If you really want to discover the reality of your own freedom—of your own self—think of it as a response to something. There is a way in which you are a 'reply' in the world. To what? A call, an invitation, a demand, a need—it can take lots of different forms. I'm not saying that human freedom is just a reply, but the key to your freedom will be the discovery in yourself of some particular capacity to respond. And in following that out you will find that you are living in the presence of the Holy One. That's the first thing. ✒ The second is the importance of the virginity of Mary. One of the essential meanings of the virginity of Mary is weakness. I've often thought that the virgin womb and the empty tomb are the same symbol: where we have no right to expect life, there is life! This virginity is not the sign of some sort of stoic restraint or a despising of the flesh. It's a sign that the response of human freedom comes out of the most unexpected places in oneself. Out of the places in yourself where you have no right to expect hope, there is a gift of response. In Mary the powerful sign of this weakness and creative power is her virginity. ✒ In us it's not the same thing. We're not simple and innocent as she was, so it's in those things in us which

are wounded and weak, those things which
are going to be transformed by forgiveness. The two places to search for the truth
of yourself, the reality of your own freedom, are in your own possibilities of response and in those places in yourself
which are like the virgin womb, places of
no apparent power and force. These might
indeed be your gifts, but in that dimension in which they go beyond your own
capacities. They might be your faults. They
might be the place of your own failures,
the place of your own fear. Somewhere
there is your own "virginity." The framework for all of this is the framework of the
Incarnation. The last word about the Incarnation in this part of the Christmas cycle
is—God enters the world by an encounter
with human freedom.

We have been talking to-
gether during the last several weeks about some of the
implications of the revelation
that God became a human
being. Today's Feast of the Epiphany closes
the Christmas cycle and leaves us with a
wonderful final image of a human life lived
as a believer. ⚜ I have already suggested that the Incarnation is not only a
revelation of what God is like, and so
necessarily, what human beings are like,
but that it is one of the ways of expressing
the very inner law of the reality in which
we live. We live in a history and in a human reality which is in some way the
enfleshing of God. How we understand
and enter into the reality of God's becoming a man in Jesus Christ will shape the
way we enter into the reality of everything
around us: the reality of money, the reality of emotional life, the reality of the
choices we have to make, the reality of
political life. ⚜ The Incarnation as the
inner law of reality does not give us a
simple superficial criterion by which to
judge all these things, but it does provide
a light by which to search into their true

depths, gradually to realize what is really going on in all the things which happen around us. It provides an horizon against which the realities of our life can take shape and achieve perspective. Everything that we experience is at its depth an experience of the Incarnation of God—now going on in the mystery of the Risen Christ. ✒

In a book I was reading last week, the author referred to that famous line of Sartre's that "Hell is other people." The writer said that this is a vivid expression of modern consciousness, that the society in which we are necessarily implicated is, in fact, a threat to us, an evil, a loss of ourselves in some way. But, he said, this is only part of Sartre's vision; "Hell is other people," all right, but we are the embodiment of other people, so in the end we are our own hell. No exit. ✒ It's that expression: "the embodiment of other people," which makes Sartre's ideas raise for us the question of the Incarnation. What are you the embodiment of? What am I the embodiment of? The image of yourself as involved in "the embodiment of God" will lead you to the truth of yourself. ✒ We're talking about the

Incarnation. Over and over again we return to it. It can be said as simply as the Christmas story can be said, but its implications go on and on and on. It is simply the most powerful image of what human life is. God became a man. ✒ As we've said before, this essential structure of all reality depends on two freedoms: God's and ours. God became flesh and continues to embody himself in a dialogue with human freedom. Somehow your freedom and mine are essential to God's entrance into human history; and the story of the Incarnation not only uncovers this fact of the role of our freedom, but also suggests something of great importance about the nature of that freedom. ✒ In the image of Mary we see that this freedom of ours has a particular characteristic: it is a response. If I am to discover the truth of my own freedom, I have to search to discover how I am a response in the world. My freedom doesn't initiate meaning all on its own. It helps to create meaning by responding to the initiative of God. ✒ Now all this can still seem very impractical and general, so abstract as not to have any existential bite into the texture of my life

as I live it day to day. This is where the
story of the Wise Men takes us a step further in grasping some of the characteristics of ourselves as a free response in the
world. If you want to think about yourself
as a freedom in the world in which God
incarnates Himself, of your life as part of
the embodiment of God, then imagine it
as a journey. Your very self—at its depth—
has the character of a journey. ✒ If all
this seems too strange a way to talk or
think—imaginative and stimulating but
unhelpful—then keep the image of the
journey of the Wise Men as background
and think about traditional religious warnings about idolatry. ✒ If we are really
to live in contact with God we cannot
settle down. This doesn't mean that our
lives are always just upset and neurotically
moving, but there is a way in which we
can settle down and stay put and so make
an idol of the particular condition in which
we find ourselves. Your freedom, which is
the freedom that responds to God, and
therefore takes part in God's actually entering human history, is a freedom which
will over and over again have to get up

and go beyond the place in which it finds

itself. Even the religious place in which it finds itself. ✒ Sometimes you will have to initiate that move, and this is a judgment you just have to learn how to make: how to discern when you have to break and move on to some further level of involvement with other people, some further commitment to service, some further search for understanding, some more study, some opening up of the experience that is prayer. If you're just settled and fixed, idolatrous, you're not responding to God in a way that is imaged by this journey. ✒ I think it's interesting that there are no details in the story of the Wise Men's journey. We're told nothing about these people before they came or about what they went back to. They exist as wanderers. And that wandering says something. Sometimes we ourselves have to respond by breaking out of where we are. Often enough the uprootings happen to us. Ordinary things happen to you in your life to move you from one settled position to another. The story of the Wise Men reminds us that in those ordinary upsetting, unsettling things we should look for a possible call from God's freedom to our freedom. That such things can be in their own way moments of God's embodiment in human history. ✒ Ordinary things. The reason I insist on the ordinary things has to do with the star. Every year at Christmas there are speculations about what the star "really was." In a way, it's funny. To our minds the journey would be true if the star were true. It's really the other way around. Since there was a journey there must have been a star. By that I mean, the thing that moved these people was something available to anybody. Anybody could have seen it. It was just there. It was an ordinary experience. It was like losing your job, or being disappointed by someone, or meeting some remarkable person, suddenly getting a new idea, menopause, even having a mind that's full of such disconnected images. ✒ Ordinary things. People moving in next door. Quite ordinary things that shift us and move us. The things where our freedom is implicated, things that terrify us, threaten us, and things that comfort us. The deepest truth about reality (any kind of reality, political, economic, personal, emotional, intellectual) is that it can become, by our

living the mysterious journey of faith, part
of the embodiment of God, the enfleshing of God.

In the Image of God

Everything about human life has the possibility of becoming a place of encounter with God. The Tradition helps make us sensitive to these possibilities and offers us wisdom about the inner patterns and structures of these ways of meeting God. The Scripture readings today (Ex 17: 8–13, 2 Tm 3: 14– 4:2, Lk 18: 1–8) draw our attention to that most basic aspect of all human experience: that we live in time, our life spread out through hours, days and years; and they suggest one of the ways that this human experience of time can become part of the interior journey of faith. ✤ All three readings are about endurance. The first thing to notice is that this is not an ethical concept; it's not the same as "patience," though on a first reading we would probably think, "Ah, yes. These are about learning patience." We are talking now about human time as a place of revelation, not as a testing ground for the development of virtue. ✤ There is, however, a close and interesting analogy between patience-as-a-virtue and endurance-as-human-time-open-to-God's-presence. I can

85

best put it negatively: impatience makes
you fragment things. If you're very impatient with somebody, you don't pay attention to the whole person. You respond
to one part and miss the rest. If you're an
impatient reader, you miss many parts of
the things you read. ✒ This brings us
round to "endurance," and to the story of
Moses in the first reading. Let the picture
become as vivid for you as possible. Don't
be impatient with the image. The image is
of an old man, Moses, standing on a hillside, overlooking a battle. This is an image of endurance, but the first thing I
would draw your attention to is that the
character Moses is only one of the characters in the story. ✒ Endurance appears
almost immediately in this story as a shared
thing. It's a matter of community. Moses'
endurance and his ability to endure does
not come out of his own strength. There
are the other figures, two young men who
are holding up the arms of this old man
standing over the battle. On his own Moses
can't do it. But we must be careful to
avoid drawing a pious and sentimental
moral. As a matter of fact, this is the very
opposite of a sentimental image. In our

terms, it's almost an immoral and blasphemous image, because there is a whole other set of figures in the story. ✍ The encounter with God is not taking place on the hillside where the weak arms of the old man are being held up by young men. The meeting with God is taking place down where people are mauling one another. While most of us would have trouble with something that in any way seems to exalt the destruction of human beings, the Scripture says the time of this war was a time of God's entering human history. ✍ We return to the image, to the intense, chaotic time of the battle and to the endurance of the figures on the hillside. In that field, where two peoples are clashing over the right to the same place, there is the fear, the horror and the blood; and above, on the hill, there is the old man whom they probably can't see, certainly don't have much time to look at, and yet to him their whole drama is connected. Endurance is an affair of community. That's the first thing; and remember that endurance is a quality in my life which allows my life to become a place where I meet God. ✍ Next I would like to mention two characteristics of our culture which militate against the development of endurance, of living in time in a way open to the discovery of God's presence. We live in a culture of the instantaneous and we live in a culture of distraction. Everybody has seen *Star Wars*, right? A perfect image of our culture is that of the space ship starting to fly at the speed of light, when it turns into light. Instantaneous everything. Instant-on television sets. Instantaneous communication. The death of one man, an entertainer, becomes part of the consciousness of almost everybody in the world almost instantaneously. Instant ways of producing things or at least very rapid ones. Instant change. It's obvious, it's a banality, but the effects of it are not banal. The most real moment in that picture was that "thump" (the space ship suddenly accelerating to the speed of light). At a very deep level we say, "Ah, that's real!" Just imagine yourself, if you can, in a culture where things grow, where what is real is what takes months to appear.

✒ Because we have a sense of reality as made up of immediate experiences and discrete bits disconnected one from the other, distraction becomes indispensable. Since nobody can live in back-to-back moments of peak experiences, what we have to do between them is, as we say (also borrowing terms from communication), tune out, relax, turn down, be distracted, disappear for a time. You see how these two aspects of our culture converge to produce our image of human time: moments of being alive separated by stretches of a kind of non-being or sleep. ↯ But is this a human time in which God can be revealed? If God is met in a life of endurance, if the sacred is encountered because of a quality of endurance (which, remember from the image, is not just me being an honorable, good, patient, private individual, but is an affair of community), if God is met there then what do we do who live in a world of the immediate and the distracting? What can we do? ↯ We come to the second reading, that reading about scripture being a source of wisdom which impregnates my consciousness so that I am aware of the encounter with God. That's an affair of endurance too, of coming back over and over again. This is a thing that an academic audience like this can understand

immediately. Those of you who are study-
ing language or literature or science know
that you don't really get in touch with
something by reading, or even by many
repeated readings when all you do is go
back to the same print. If every time you
picked up some work of music or scientific
theory, you just thought the same thing
about it, there would be no penetration
of it. You would not touch the reality or
the depths of it.   ✥   When we read
Scripture, the same thing could happen.
To say that Scripture is a source of wisdom is not to say that what I now think
about it is a source of wisdom or what
you think about it is a source of wisdom.
It's to say that if we return over and over
again with this kind of endurance, there is
hidden there a source of wisdom.   ✥   So
we come back to ourselves, celebrating the
Eucharist together Sunday after Sunday.
We are, as a group, a wonderful instance
of contemporary society with a vengeance.
All together and all alone. We're like a
bunch of atoms floating around. You experience during the prayer, I'm sure you
do (I do every Sunday), the intensity of
the personal life here and the disconnect-

edness of it.   ↯   What if you approach
other people with a sense that they have
strengths which you require, like the old
man hovering over the battle, or that you
have strengths that they require; that somehow or other our strengths and weakness
should not repel us from one another but
become places of meeting with the Holy,
that we see them as a source of mutual
endurance? How do we talk to one another? How do we talk to one another
after Mass here? Are we for one another a
distraction, a source of distraction? Is that
the quality of our listening? Or are we for
one another a possible source of wisdom?
Do I come into this room thinking,
"Somebody's going to say something to
me today that has to be attended to, kept,
remembered?"   ↯   It's a horrible thing
to think of really, for people who have
lived through this much of the twentieth
century, that any religion could say that
God is present where human beings are
slaughtering and mauling and mutilating
one another, but that's the image we have
to deal with.   ↯   In the silence, I think it
might be good to go back into that image, to let it become vivid. The image of

the presence of God in the world: an old
man supported in a position often used to
express blessing, somewhat suggesting a
cross—and impregnating a battle with the
presence of God. God is there. If that is a
way the Holy enters the world, what are
the possibilities for the way the Holy enters your world or mine?

We begin to enter the mystery of the Eucharist this morning by remembering all of the stories that are converging in this place, our own story first of all. God will become present under the sacramental signs of bread and wine in this community because He is already present under so many other signs and so many other realities in the story of each one of us. What we do here is a celebration of faith, not magic. It's a repossession of our own life in faith, reminding ourselves that our story is now part of the mystery of Christ's love for the Father. Just looking around us, we can realize how many kinds of stories are present here. And it's not just us. Think about how many people are implicated in this Eucharist through us. We never come to the Eucharist alone.

At its heart, a life of faith centers around a particular sort of attentiveness. This attentiveness is not just a question of your mind. It's a very complex total presence of yourself to your own experience. If you were going to break up the characteristics of this attentiveness into different dimensions of human life, it would also include a kind of willingness, a readiness to move beyond the limits of your own experience. ✒ Kierkegaard called this a kind of risk, a leap beyond the boundaries of ourselves, of yourself as you've been constructed by your experience, or as you have constructed yourself, beyond the limits of your own choices. This attentiveness will involve a leap beyond all this because by its very nature it includes *loving*. It includes feelings. It includes the experience of being acted upon as well as acting. But at the heart of the matter the life of faith is a kind of attention, and without this attentiveness the business of being a believer, being really a believer in a whole human life, is impossible. ✒ Being a believer is a way of being human. It means living every ordinary part of human life as a possible place of meeting with God. The essential key to living this way is attention, and that's why the practice of prayer, in which we learn to pay attention in this way, is indispensable to living as a believer. The key is that kind of attentiveness which brings us down beneath the surface of other people, of events, of parts of our own self to that place where they become

a place of meeting with God. 🌿 We
must learn to be attentive in this way because the God we're going to meet is God
as He really is, the Holy One who really
is. 🌿 The three readings (Acts 14:
21–27; Rv 21: 1–5; Jn 13: 31–35) sum-
marize the whole of the Christian life. You
have in the first reading a very simple, in
fact, *dull*, recitation of places where people
began to live together in Christian com-
munities. If it were being written now on
Long Island, they would have mentioned
Northport, Bay Shore, Stony Brook. They
just happened to be named Galatia, Cap-
padocia, Bithynia. 🌿 When we hear
that reading, it sounds odd. And I think
that's an interesting thing. That is, they
are ordinary places where ordinary people
gathered, and yet they are strange and special places; both things are true about the
Christian experience. Because if you really
take the ordinariness of another person
seriously, it's strange. Your ordinariness is
what is concrete and particular about you.
It's an ordinary story, this business of finding yourself in a Christian community. And
yet it has all of the quality of strangeness
that any human life, taken seriously, really

has. Any human life. Including your own.
🖋 The core, the core of the truth of the
whole business, is in the second reading.
The God whom you really meet is the
God who creates. The key line is at the
end: the one on the throne spoke and
said, "Now I am making, in the whole of
creation, something new." That is the God
who creates, the God who from moment
to moment makes something as radically
original as *something* as opposed to *nothing*. The radical appearance of being out
of nothingness. Creation is the radical appearance of history out of chaos. 🖋
The God you're going to meet is the God
who, in the ordinary things of your experience, of my experience, is creating something radically original. And that's why the
attentiveness is crucial. If we're going to
live a life of faith, it has to be a meeting
between our freedom and God's freedom.
But the originality comes from God's side.
If you're going to meet the truth of Him,
you're going to have to pay attention
enough to what is happening so that you
are not trying to impose your own freedom on God but are beginning to live in
contact with what is really going on. 🖋

How do people learn to make music, what is at the heart of all that study and re-hearsing? Isn't it that they pay enough at-tention to what is there (and notice how every part of themselves and everything that has gone on in their lives is involved in this) until they can re-create the origi-nality of the one who created the music in the first place? That's a good image for what I am trying to talk about. ✒ At the heart of the matter is God's radical act of creation, which is going on in the most ordinary dimensions of your life. If you're going to be able to join that act of crea-tion, which is eventually going to involve the kind of risk that Kierkegaard talked about, the going-beyond the limits of where you already are (and there's noth-ing automatic about joining it, because it is an act of freedom on our part), if we're going to be able to do that, it's got to be rooted in an attention which reaches un-derneath to the heart of things to be in the presence of their reality. ✒ When you are in the presence of the reality of another person, you're in the presence of God. That other person is a creature; and there is, between the Creator and the creature, the intimacy that there is between the singer and the song. They are as close to being identical as they can be without being identical. When you're *really* in the presence of the reality of *anything*, you're in the presence of God. ✒ At the heart of the matter of living a life of faith is this kind of attentiveness. It's rooted in the truth of Creation. Creation is one of the fundamental Christian categories. It names the way God is present in what is not God. When Saint Paul tried to find a category to say what was happening in Jesus Christ he couldn't find anything better than to call it "a new creation." ✒ What you're doing, then, when you're living a Christian life, is this: at different times you're paying attention to different aspects of your own life, led by your experience, by your interests, by your stage of life, by the kind of sensitivity you have, by whatever God is doing to you at the time. You're paying attention to different aspects of your own life until you reach that point where they become a meeting with God. ✒ The aspect that's pointed to in the third reading, the aspect that can make of human experience a place of meeting with

God, is love. (Don't slip into your habitual ways of thinking about this, especially when you hear "love" used in pious contexts like this. And don't narrow its meaning to the modern notion of romantic love.) The reading is saying that if there is affection among you, if you find love among you, that is a sign that God is there. Love in any of its dimensions, attraction to one another, interest in one another, service of one another, passion for one another, patience with one another, puzzlement about one another. (You can add on, I'm just making these up as I go.) If there is a group which finds itself in love in any of its dimensions, and if you're attentive enough to that love, you can move to the heart of a life of faith. ✒ The love itself is not God. We can turn that love in on itself, believe that what we have experienced of it is its whole truth, that there's nothing beyond what we already know, no wisdom beyond what we already have. Just to rest within it, whether it's the love of one other person and the comfort that brings us, or a small group of people who give us a sense of security or interest or talent or whatever it is; *or* you can take the second reading seriously and believe that this small group of people is a place where the Holy One is creating something radically new among us. If we pay enough attention to it. The whole of the adventure of faith is in these three readings. If you pay attention enough to your own *sin*, for that matter, you can find God in it. If you don't pay attention enough to your own sin all you find is yourself. (Which is where you were in the first place.) If you pay attention you can find in your sinfulness the God who forgives.   ✒️   If you attend to your own love you will find God, and finding God will mean that you will be drawn into the incredible vortex of a new creation. The heart of the matter is God's freedom. God's freedom meets your freedom. The adventure of faith takes place where God's freedom meets your freedom.

If you were to try to say, very simply, what Christianity is all about—if you were trying to express to somebody who had never been in contact with it what is the heart of being a Christian, I think you'd say something like this: Christianity is about concentrating all of yourself, all of your life, everything in you that can be focused, that can move, everything in you that can recognize, learn and love, concentrating yourself, on the mystery of Jesus Christ. What makes Christianity a particular way of living in the world is the possession of your self by the mystery of Jesus.   It is like being in love with someone. The stories of the focusing of human lives on Jesus or the possession of these lives by Him are very different from each other. Our loving is different. Our capacity to love, the way we love, what we love with—our minds, or our feelings, or our passions or our hope or our bodies. We love differently.   Christianity would make no sense unless it is possible to do what I've just described *really*, and not just in our imagination. And the only thing that makes that possible is the

Resurrection, that the mystery of Jesus (the reason I don't just want to say the person of Jesus, I'll come to in a minute) is really present in the human story. It is really possible, as possible as it would be, say, for you to love me, for you to love the mystery of Jesus. To be completely in love with Christ. Not just to think about something that happened once in human history. Not just to plan for something that may happen within the cosmos again. It is really possible for you to focus your whole being on Him now. ✒ The reason I'm avoiding saying "on the person of Jesus" is that, while being in love with Jesus is *like* being in love with an individual, it is not the same. Jesus is not a physical, individual man now, so that, for instance, to be in love with Him would exclude being in love with others. When you focus your whole life, when you make of yourself *totally* a gift of love, when you fall in love with the love that is Christ, it is not something that stands between you and other people, or takes the place of other people, but it is a reality that binds you to them. It is, for us, the only way really to love others. ✒ For thousands of years individual women and men have gradually discovered in the story of their lives what it means for them to be in love with Christ and to be loved by Him. How did this discovery take place? A lot like the discovery of human loving, it occurs when many different parts of ourselves and moments of our lives come together to a point of realization, "Yes, I love her." "Yes, I love these people and this place." At that point of convergence we grasp something about the very core of ourselves, the creative center that is myself as an original freedom in the world, able to decide, to dream, to give myself to something. ✒ This dimension of our own human reality—this self—can become a place of meeting with Christ only in prayer. The crucial discovery of being loved and of your capacity to love Jesus Christ comes in holding yourself at this creative center (not out at the edges of your self and the bits and pieces of your life) in the presence of the mystery of God. The solitude of attentive prayer is a very uncomfortable and even frightening place for all of us, but it is crucial if we are to reach the heart of the matter: to love Jesus Christ. It is also crucial if we are not to construct our religious life around idols of our own imagining. ✒ There is another place in yourself where this meeting with the mystery of Christ can take place, which was pointed to in last week's reading (Jon 3:1–5): your ability to repent, to find a way past the limits which have built themselves into your life. ✒ Repentance has to do with breaking into something unexpectedly new. It does not have to do with being sad about what you've done. That's remorse, not repentance. Repentance means finding in the weakness and the woundedness of your life (since sin is a very social phenomenon, it could very well be what the sin of other people has done to you as well as the sin that you've fashioned for yourself) to find there a hopeful breaking into something new. ✒ Repentance has to do with finding in your own hatred and pettiness and self-centeredness the capacity for a new life. I mentioned to you last week that if you want to examine your life for a place of repentance, to live with yourself at that depth, use the Beatitudes. They're the surest key I know of to where repentance can happen. Find where the gift of being poor is real for you. The gift of making peace. The gift of suffering with other people. The gift of being thirsty for justice. You'll find yourself breaking into the story of Christ because the Beatitudes are in fact another way of describing the mystery of Jesus. They are His "biography." ✒ In fact the discovery of your gift of repentance is a sign that you've met the Risen Christ, the One who can bring life out of the place of death. It is only a heart transformed by repentance that allows us to love the mystery of Jesus Christ with our whole being. ✒ One last point. Suppose we were not Christian, suppose we were Buddhists and you were here saying, "Look, I want to seek transformation— what do I do? What's the first step? Where do I go to look? What do I do with my body, and the food I use and things like that?" You would get an answer. You would be told about meditation. You would be told about the discipline of yoga. A Christian says to you: "Being a Christian is being in love with the mystery of Jesus." Where do you go with that really? Where is the principal place you go with that? You go to history. Human history. To be a Christian means to plunge into the reality of history. And when I'm talking about history I'm talking about change and development. What has been redeemed by Jesus? The human story has been redeemed. Something is going on in human history which is going to lead to our transformation in the mystery of God.

🖋 The place where you meet Jesus is not in disengaged meditation. The place where you are able to fall in love and to discover yourself to be loved is not just at the core of your being—though that's a very important thing. It is in the real story of what is now going on in the real world.

🖋 You want to know who Christ is for you? Ask yourself what's going on in the real world around you and where you belong in that story. It may be a very small world. It may be two, three, four, five people. It may be people in the dorm. It may be people in your family. It may be a larger world. You ask yourself now and answer that question with all your imagination, all your attentiveness. How do you get into history really? By taking small things seriously. By having a respect for the particular and the practical. By not letting yourself float off into distraction, instant gratification, ideas. ✒️ You want to get into history? The real history of what's really going on? Of course you'll make mistakes about what it is. Of course you'll do all kinds of dumb and stupid and wrong things. But if you want to be there where Christ is, if you want to know, in truth, what it means for you to fall in love with love, with God, to be completely focused on that love, begin to ask yourself: "What's going on really around me? What is really happening? And where do I fit? Who are the other characters who are important right now in my story?"

You can best listen to what I will try to say this evening if you imagine it as bits and pieces of a leisurely conversation among friends. Not a set piece, a homily or a class lecture, but ideas tried out, suggestions to be taken up again. I have often wondered, in fact, if it is not so that Christianity can only truthfully be talked about the way friends talk to friends. ✿ The readings (Jb 7: 1–4, 6, 7; I Cor 9: 16–19; Mk 1: 29–39) present us today with three fascinating human figures: Jesus, Paul and Job. Let's talk about how they are bound up with one another, involved with the same reality—the presence of God in human history. ✿ Certainly in Western literature, perhaps in any literature, Job is the figure who most vividly expresses the depths and terror of human suffering and abandonment. If you recall the first reading: hopelessness. That's what Job is. He is hopeless, and he has been delivered over to this hopelessness in some way with God's agreement. ✿ Then there is Paul. He's a genius, a creative genius, a religious genius, an organizational genius— and he is an awful pain to a lot of people, a puzzlement to a great many people. There are echoes of it in the Epistles. "Can you believe Paul and not abandon Christ?" Paul has to trust his vision. He cannot live the way the others lived. (Many of the Apostles apparently stayed in families, were supported by other people.) Paul cannot live the way others do—and yet he is extraordinarily adaptable. More adaptable, it seems, than Peter. Paul could really live as part of Roman culture and as part of Jewish culture; so much so, that people accused him of being a turncoat and a fraud. His answer is fascinating: he'll be anything, anywhere with everybody, in the hopes that *some* will be saved. He recognizes that he will never see the acceptance of what he knows to be true by all these people whom he loves so passionately. And he goes on.

Finally, the figure of Jesus. Today's reading shows him passing through a village—one of dozens in his life—and He is God, Divine Being passing through human history with the power to heal. And when he left, there were still people suffering. These three figures are linked at the heart of the matter of human life where most of us do not want to stay.

If religious people believe that human reality can be a place of meeting with God,
then this is surely one of the indispensable
places of meeting—this core of human life
where life and death, vision and failure,
love and inability to love are always present.
ᶳ To be a Christian is to stay there
where these painfully contrasting dimensions of human life really are, and to *believe*, to risk your life that in the final word
it is life and not death that is true. In the
last of it, it is love and not hate that is
true. Jesus Christ passed through a place
and when he left there were still people
suffering and there was still death. ᶳ
Christianity is about enduring in the choice
that life has the last word and not death,
even though you don't see it—and won't
see it. And, like Paul, you can endure in a
choice that says, "I will do all these things
and some people may recognize it." ᶳ
It is hard to endure being human. It is
hard to endure other people's being human too. Maybe harder. Religious people
who dream of pie in the sky by and by,
and the atheistic humanist who rejects such
a crazy dream and says, "I will settle for
what there is here and now," are both

making the same response. Both of them are refusing to endure with life and death together, and choosing life.   ✒ I said before that being a Christian is like being in love. It is being in love with God. With Jesus, God in flesh. It's played out by being in love with other people, and that's where all the difficulty comes. Enduring. Believing in your own ability to love in the face of what for you is unlovable.   ✒ We come back to the three figures: Job, who is presented to us this morning just in the dark pictures (there are a lot of other things in Job), just that; Paul, defending himself, which is what this part of the letter is about, defending his own vision, and in the middle of it acknowledging that his vision, on which he's wagered his life, will not be shared by most people, and still loving them. This really should be talked about the way friends talk because this is not meant to be big formal ideas. It's meant to be the kind of thoughts that happen in conversation. And Jesus. What happened to Christ? What was going on when He was all alone in prayer? Why didn't the Gospel writers put down what went on in His prayer? Why did they say nothing about that except that He was there? 🖌 Maybe because for us who are following Him, all we need to know is that there's a place like that for us too. Whether you find it in long periods of silence or in little bits and pieces. Wherever you find it. Where you come to your own choosing of life. Where you come to your own endurance. Choosing and endurance and all those other words (choosing love rather than hate) come down to a final question, "Can you discover yourself as a lover of other human beings, and which ones?"

In the Image of God

Among the many wonderful things the 18th and 19th centuries have given us, there are also some unterrific things that we've inherited from that time. One of these is the difficulty we have hearing the things we've heard today: the reading (Gn 22) about Abraham on the mountain binding his son to sacrifice; the reading (Mk 9) about Jesus on the mountain with his disciples, His transfiguration, an awesome presence breaking through into ordinary reality. It's very hard for us to hear those things with a sense of their truth. If we try to make any sense of them at all, to give them value, we tend either to psychologize or to moralize them.

I'd just like to ask you to stay awhile in the presence of those two extraordinary, terrifying images. What's going on? What's happening? Who is really there? Who is on that mountain with Abraham, a man sacrificing his son? Even as we recoil from the idea of such an act, we realize that he's doing more than sacrificing his son: he's killing his future. He's killing his own hope. What's going on there? What can it mean to say that this was an encounter with God? ✒ There is a reality into which human reality is plunged. We are, in fact, involved with something real and enormous, which in part has to do with darkness and terror, and the hope and the strangeness of that story of Abraham and his son and God. ✒ As I was thinking about this story, I realized that I was trying to be a mere spectator, but such a story doesn't have any mere spectators. The hope. The darkness. The strange demand that can come to me from reality. ✒ And what really happened on that other mountain? What is it like to be in the presence of a God who loves you and me so much that He identifies Himself in that way with us? Why at the moment when there is the splendor of God, so unimaginably present in human form that flesh becomes light...at that moment when there really is divine revelation, why is there talk of the most weak of human things? The most scary of human things? The most, really, disgusting of human things? Death. ✒ What is it like to be in the presence of a God whose inner being is to love us so much, not as we might be, not as we will become when we're all trans-

formed, but to love human beings, love
the people on your corridor, even them,
even yourself? What is it like to be in the
presence of such a God?   There are a
couple of reasons why we attempt to re-
main spectators in these two stories. First
of all, we just don't take ourselves seriously enough, we don't respect ourselves
enough. I don't respect you enough. If
the story about Abraham and the killing
of hope is true of every human being, how
serious a thing a human life is! What a
respectful thing it is!   For us, however, there is too much distraction from
our real self. It's true. We don't take ourselves seriously enough. You might think
the most important thing about you is that
you're going to make money. You don't
take yourself seriously enough, your *self*
involved in these two stories. Not that
making money and having careers doesn't
have some meaning. But they're not the
whole of you.   I don't take myself
seriously enough. I worry about a lot of
trivial things. I distract myself in so many
ways. That's the first thing. Distraction. I
think we do not touch the truth of these
stories because we're too distracted.

The second reason—really the other side of the first—we're too distracted because we're terrified.... What separates us from one another is the same thing that makes us recoil from that story of Abraham: We're horrified by the confrontation with death and evil that is in that story. We're scared to death of our own evil and of the evil in others; and we're scared of one another's death. Maybe the only way to take ourselves *really* seriously is to love us as God loves us, which involves acknowledging the whole story, and all the parts of the story of our lives. ✒ The day before yesterday when I woke up I had a very sharp, clear, hard image of myself. I use all those adjectives because they unite.... I saw myself very clearly and completely unsympathetically. I saw, I think, very clearly what I look like to somebody who doesn't have the same goodwill toward me as I would wish you would have toward me. And what I realized about myself was true, and it was deadening. It was literally a murderous image of myself. I was thinking that I sometimes have that kind of image of other people. The vision I have of them and had of myself at that mo-

ment was murderous. *Is* murderous. It kills
the life in them. I don't mean this to be a
sentimental plea, "Oh, look on the bright
side of people. Look on the bright side of
yourself." What I saw is the truth. I certainly know what I saw about myself *is* the
truth. ✒ And yet there is another possibility. I have been looked at with a vision
that is truthful and not murderous. With a
vision that is truthful and creative. It's not
something you can simply choose to do,
to see yourself as you appear to the Holy
One, to the one whom Jesus calls Father,
to Infinite Love. The first step toward this
vision of ourselves includes a kind of choice
or, better, a refusal. The murderous, fear-
ful vision we have of one another is in
some way our own creation, and we can
refuse it. ✒ I can't by my own choice
see either myself or you as God sees us, as
we really are. But I can refuse my own
idols. Refusing my own creation, I can
wait in hope for the gift of entering God's
creation. And I think this refusal of our
own illusions is the first step by which we
enter the hopeful mystery of the Eucharist: as we live from the Eucharist we begin slowly to have a vision of human beings

through the eyes of Jesus Christ, the Dead and Risen One, and first of all, a vision of ourselves through those eyes.

I don't have a fully developed homily. I have the idea out of which I would develop a homily, so I'll just give you the idea and you can develop the homily yourself. 🖋 The idea is about the Incarnation: an attempt to identify that in us to which the Incarnation of Jesus Christ is a response. Or, to put it a slightly different way, that in us to which the Incarnation of God is announced. All through Advent our attention is called to a characteristic of being human, which we know in ourselves as individuals, but which becomes more profound and important when we think about our lives connected to one another. 🖋 We experience a kind of malaise which affects that which is most deeply true about us. It affects our ability to know and especially to know one another—to know other people and their works and their creations, to know ourselves even. That ability to know, to know the meanings of things, not just to endure things but in some way to understand them. To touch their center regardless of whether those things are wonderful: the beginning of life, falling in love, coming to discover a truth; or whether they're terrible: the destruction of a people, enduring of war or the approach of death and pain. ✍ This malaise also affects our ability to be genuine companions of one another, to love and to accept love. Being a human being is somehow wounded and dark. You experience it differently from the way I do. Each human being experiences it in her own way, the darkness of it. ✍ That which we all know on the level of human experience points to something which we cannot experience directly, but which is mirrored in this malaise which affects our deepest self. There is something very, very wrong between us and God. We are profoundly separated from the Being with whom we should be most deeply in communion. Now, it's that reality in human life to which the Incarnation is announced, that part of ourselves which is meant to hear that God took human flesh. That's the first part of the idea. ✍ The second part of the idea is what the Incarnation says about this human situation of wounded knowing and wounded loving. Human beings have always been aware of

this rupture, this distance which ought not
to be there between us and Divine Being,
however they name God or understand
God. And they have always tried to re-
establish communion where there is this
isolation. What the Incarnation says today
is that the answer from the side of God is
a new act of creation, a new level of being,
a capacity in Jesus, in God-made-man, and
then in all of us because of our mystical
union with Him. ✒ He wanted no
sacrifice or oblation (the ways we have
struggled to create this communion). He
took no pleasure in holocausts for sin. And
then I said, "Here I am, I am coming to
do Your will, to love you and to know
and to love other women and men." That
is the word of the Incarnation. It is now
possible.

In the Image of God

The gift of wisdom is puzzling and paradoxical, and you're only going to reach its meaning slowly and by a kind of patient testing of what God has done with you so far. Wisdom is another name for God, so when you're talking about the gift of wisdom, you're talking about a particular kind of intimate presence of God in your life. ⚘ But this is a presence that has to do with thinking, with having some idea of what things mean, of what they're for, of what's happening to you, what the possibilities are before you, what the real possibilities are for your future, what the real meanings are that are hidden in your past. ⚘ Wisdom is about those things. The world is beyond us, indeed our very self is beyond us. Most of us who are alive nowadays are aware that we don't understand a whole lot of what's happening. In fact, we have borne in on us a sense of being overwhelmed both by information and by knowledge, and by suggestions of realms beyond realms of reality. Relativity theory suggests a world in which we can't even imagine ourselves living, but it says that's

the one we really live in. Psychological in-
sights keep suggesting that there are depths
inside depths so that you scarcely know
any part of yourself for which you can say,
"Well, I'm really responsible for that. I
know what's happening. I know what I'm
doing and why I'm doing it." We're people
very much aware that it's hard to claim a
lot of wisdom about all these things. ✒

So what are we talking about when we say
that God promises those who believe—
who risk their lives on the truth of what
happened to Jesus Christ—a gift of wisdom? I'll say it again: being a believer is
not a way of escaping being human, it's
not a way of avoiding the bewilderment
and limitation of our own time. It is a way
of being human. To believe in the Resurrection is not a way of escaping death; it is
a way of dying. ✒ And that brings us
back to "wisdom". For us Christians, the
cross is the ultimate symbol of wisdom. In
the very physical image of the cross is hidden the most significant wisdom about the
possibilities of my life, about the meanings of what has happened to me already.
One of the important expressions about
the wisdom of the cross is here, in Luke

14: 25–33: "Unless you take up your cross and follow me, you cannot be where I am, you cannot experience what I experience." ✒ Now, like the line, "Give away everything you own," the *obvious* meaning of this from Luke is clearly not the *real* meaning of it. Jesus is not saying here that there's trouble in the world and don't try to run away from it. Everybody knows there's trouble in the world. In fact, you can't escape trouble. ✒ If you try to live a life absolutely devoid of trouble and difficulty and struggle, then you're obviously a fool. But you don't need divine revelation to know that. All you need is to live long enough and look around to see what kind of superficial and silly person that would be. In fact, the primary meaning of the cross for a believer is not pain. The cross means pain to everybody. *Anybody*, believer or unbeliever, looking at the cross can tell that that's an image of suffering and pain. What does it mean when you look at the cross and see it as a revelation of God? The wisdom of the Cross is not the fact of Jesus' suffering, but that in the suffering, this Man dead on the wood is an expression of what God is like, is an image of the place in human experience where God is met. ⚡ I'm certainly not going to say that the cross is the key to *all* wisdom and now tell you what the cross means. I don't even know what it means for myself, and I'm not arrogant enough to tell you what it means for you; but I can suggest one place where that kind of meaning can come for you. And I'm going to do that by a story, which may not seem to be connected to all this, but it is. ⚡ I was talking to a friend of mine yesterday about another friend of mine, both of them people my age, solidly middle-aged. One of them has just learned from his doctor that he's got a congenital heart defect, and that his doctors are considering open heart surgery to fix up the heart, if that's possible to do. The other one, the one who was talking to me about it, is an atheist. The guy with the bad heart is a Catholic. The atheist said to me, "I don't know if surgery is the answer. I had a congenital kidney defect, and when I was twenty they operated on it to correct it and it didn't work, and then I had another operation and another and they finally took my kidney out." Then he said,

"I think we're much too mechanistic. We keep thinking of the body as a machine. The carburetor's bad, we tinker with it. If it stays bad, we take it out and put in another one. Maybe having a congenital heart defect is saying something about all of us and about the way we live. Maybe we should live with less stress *with* the congenital heart defect instead of trying to tinker with the machine."   ✹   The wisdom of the Cross is not contained in the pain of the cross, but rather in this, that the cross was an expression of some profound communion between Jesus and His Father for which we have no other words than "the cross." There isn't any other better way to say it. There is no more powerful symbol. There isn't anything that would express it more vividly. But you can't enter into it, be *really* in the presence of it, if you're still on the outside saying, "Oh, that's awful. Oh, isn't that sad," or feeling very sentimental or guilty. If you're in the presence of the Cross, you are in the presence of the most radical key to what binds you to God, to Christ, to other people.   ✹   Unless you take up your cross every day, you relate to others only as people who need help or bother you or help you or delight you. That's all. You experience your troubles, pains, fears as bad times that you have. That's all. But is your life just something to be tinkered with, or can it be lived as if it's the presence of something more? How do you live it as if it's the presence of something more? That's very hard to say. But there is a threshold to be crossed. A crucial threshold, which is expressed by the Cross. You have a gift of wisdom. You didn't earn it, so you can't lose it. There is nothing you could do to have thrown it away. It is the presence of God. There is some way in which God is drawing you into that circle of His own life. Infinite knowledge and infinite love draw me, you, as we really are, into the circle. ✒ The things that are happening to us are part of that being drawn in. So, with just the image of the cross as vivid to you as you can make it, just a cross, let your life be present to you. If you see your life or some part of it as a taking up of the cross, that does not mean doing hard things. It does not mean looking at the troubles you have. It means, within the hard things, *or* the good ones, raising the question of how you are most deeply bound to other people. Or whatever else the mystery of the cross might mean for you. To put the two together, you not only have a gift of wisdom, you have a *gift* to take up the cross.

In the Image of God

The very fact of being a human being involves the most profound kind of contradictory realities. We are beings who think, create art, make language, can love; beings almost unbelievably gifted and splendid. At the same time we digest food, excrete, gradually decay, and all die. We're free, and we are inescapably restricted and bound. We can actually make *new* things, begin new kinds of ideas, new political realities, new technologies; and at the same time we're bound by determinism and coded at birth with all kinds of biological necessities, limited by all kinds of psychological givens.

✥ Try to get as vividly as you can an image of what it is to be human, perhaps with the emphasis on those aspects of being human which puzzle you, give you a sense of limitation, terrify you, make you want to deny them. It's against that background that Christianity holds up its vision of God.

✥ Christianity (and Christmas reminds us of this particularly) is a crazy religion. Very important! It is a mad and shocking religion. We're no longer shocked by it because we have become accustomed to

it, just as we're not usually shocked by being human; although when we start thinking about being human we realize just how shocking it really is. Christianity is an embarrassing religion. ✒ Christianity says that God became a human being. This is not a claim that there was once a man who in a quite mysterious way was transformed into the presence of God in the world, a man who learned the secret of transforming human reality into that of companion and instrument of Divine Being. This would be a splendid and challenging and ultimately imaginable religious vision. But the Christian vision is not ultimately imaginable in that way. Christianity claims that the Divine, Infinite Creator of the universe became a human being, with all of the limitedness which is involved in being human; that the Infinite Creator of the universe became someone with a particular temperament. One who had to learn. Whom some people liked and some people didn't. Who had limits, probably, to what he liked and didn't. ✒ Think of it in the ways that we hardly ever do: if you asked, "What was there in Jesus?" you'd say, "A human being." But if you ask, "Who was there?" you must say, "The Son of God." Who died? In his human nature, the son of God. Whom did people like or not like? ✒ In trying to get yourself to live in the presence of this astounding vision of God and of reality and of yourself, you have to break out of some things that have grown limited in you. The images go in all sorts of directions. I'm not good at geometry, but if there is a geometry that goes in all sorts of directions, it would make a good model. You have to break up, break out, break in. You have to break into greater depths of yourself in order to be in the presence of this faith. You have to break out of certain ways which have limited you from standing in the presence of reality, break out of certain illusions. You have to break into the lives of other people. All of this exploding out and up and in and down are images of what we call repentance. ✒ Repentance takes place in those dimensions of your life that are limited and fixed and dead, those things which have happened to you through other people or through yourself which bind you in certain ways. They are the places of moral impossibility.

135

Repentance happens in the places where you are incapable of life. Where you're incapable of loving, or incapable of working, or incapable of daring to act. Incapable of appreciating something in others. Where you're incapable of *not* being afraid. ✒ In those places which have become places of incapacity and limit there is a breaking out, a breaking out of the illusion that the limits are the final reality. We call that breakout "repentance." The reason I say that repentance must happen in order for us even to listen to the story of God becoming a human being is that when God acts, we are never spectators. God's action always involves our freedom. His action is not like a film, that is, something from which I am disconnected, which I simply see. When God acts it is much more like meeting with another human being. It's like being spoken to. Running into somebody. Suddenly finding yourself in the face of something. It's like a work of art in whose presence you have to respond. ✒ God's actions are always creative, in some way, of myself, my freedom. So, if I'm going even to think about God becoming a man in Jesus, I

have to reach some level of myself, to be
alive in a certain way. And the way you
get to that kind of life is through
repentance. ✍ What is repentance like?
If you're repenting about something, what
is the "mood" you find yourself in? (But
it's something deeper than a mood.) What
is the *quality* of repentance? If you're going
to look for the possibility of repentance,
where it can happen in you, right now,
then what is that quality in yourself that
you're looking for? Think about the word
"hope." If you want to know what you're
doing when you're repenting, or how you
begin to repent, discover what the possibilities of hopefulness are for you. That
breaking out, breaking in, breaking down;
that reaching of a greater depth in yourself which is repentance is an interior journey of hope. If you really journey to the
depths of yourself (or of any thing or person), you will find yourself in the presence
of God. You don't create the presence of
God, you discover it. God entering human history is not something that we have
to work up to. It's the truth that we have
to come into the presence of. And we come
into the presence of it by hope. If you can

imagine your life bathed in hope even a little bit, you know what it means to be repentant. ❧ Right now think about somebody else, or about some part of your life that's really dead, fixed, limited, dark, wounded; and think about living that part of yourself or living with somebody else, hopefully. That doesn't mean that you think about other things. Hope doesn't make you think about other things. Hope doesn't mean dreaming of something else that's going to happen. That's hopelessness. When you've given up on something you start thinking about something else. Suppose you say to somebody who's dying that we are going to be hopeful. It's going to make you pay more attention to her. When you're hopeless about her, you try to think about something else. ❧ The places within ourselves where we have to change in order to enter the truth of this story, this incredible story of God becoming human, are the places where we have to repent. That is to say, the places where we can begin to be hopeful about ourselves. Hopefulness, this hope I'm talking about, is not itself something that you have to create. It's not a psychological state.

It's not the opposite of being depressed, for instance. You can be depressed and hopeful at the same time. You can be joyous and hopeful at the same time. You can be sad and in the midst of disaster and be hopeful at the same time. ✍ Hopefulness has to do with entering the depths of what's really there. Breaking through the illusions. Opening yourself up to the reality that is not of your making but which speaks to your freedom: the entrance of God into your life. ✍ If the story of God becoming man is true, then if you put yourself into the presence of that truth, no matter how long and dark and twisted the journey is going to be for you to live this hope, this hopefulness, you will find God active there. If it is true that there is God, and that God enters human life, then it's *not* something that we have to make up. It's something that we have to get ourselves in touch with. What the story of John the Baptist and these others suggest is just that the ways in which I'm *not* in touch with the truth of God-in-human-flesh are the ways in which I'm living without hope. To begin to be hopeful about yourself, or to begin to be hopeful about somebody else, will raise those questions, for *you*, to which the incarnation of God is the response.... If I can imagine myself bathed in hopefulness, what do I begin to sense in myself? Think about the person you live with, or some people you work with, but think about them hopefully, and see where it leads you.

I want to talk about Lent. I think the most vivid single line about Lent is in the story of Moses talking to the people right after the covenant had been entered into with God (Dt 30: 15–20). He says to them, "I put before you today death and life. *Choose life.*" That's what Lent is about. You have the choice before you. You always have it before you—but Lent is the time we recognize that this choice is at the heart of the matter of being human. ✒ I put before you death and life. Choose life. But remember that you *can* choose death. That's a real possibility. And it's a possibility not only at just one moment or another, but it's the possibility of the whole story of your life. There's no simple way around that. It's not just a matter of doing this or that. It's not just a matter of having good intentions. Human life is an extraordinarily complex and profound adventure. In Jesus, one human life was enough to express the inner life of God. ✒ *Choosing.* Being presented with death or life is not like being presented Fords or Chevys. This choice is not just a selection between

two external possibilities. What is the
choosing of life like if it's not at all like
selecting between objects we can consume,
or other choices which are clearly defined?
❧ I would suggest that it is more like
remembering. In fact, crucial to the choosing of life is the ability to remember your
own story, to keep before you those things
which will be the elements of the decision. It's more like uncovering illusions
and freeing yourself from them than it is
like choosing to buy something or to travel
to some place. There is decision in it, but
it's not the simple deciding to do this or
that, or *not* to do this or that. In fact, the
choice of life frequently takes place only
within death, as we'll see in a moment.
❧ What *is* life, as Moses uses the word?
Why would anyone confronted with life
and death choose death? Choosing life has
more to do with creating something. It's
closer to active artistic creation than anything else: making of one thing the presence of something more than itself. We
find ourselves now, perhaps, for the first
time in history, experiencing life as being
made up of different and separable parts.

Physical life can be opposed to conscious

life, to individual life. ✒ To those who wrote the Bible, it was unthinkable that an individual would imagine her own reality as isolated from everyone else. It was unthinkable that the life of the body and the life of the spirit could be separated. We now can think such things. With technology we can do such things. So now people search for the "quality of life". I wonder if this isn't an expression of vaguely remembering what life is, of remembering that life has to do with connections and wholeness. It's like nostalgia in somebody who has amnesia. You have a feeling of sadness and loss, but you don't even know what it is you've forgotten. ✒ Choosing life—This choosing of life is actually a choice of our true self. This is a choice we can make only in the presence of God, which is why Moses presented the challenge at the moment of sealing the covenant. We can be in the presence of our true self only in the presence of God; we can serve life (and not illusion) only in the presence of the One Who creates life. That's the truth. That's what Lent is about. ✒ Let me go around and say it a slightly different way. Liturgically, as you know,

Lent is a preparation for Easter. In the early centuries of the Christian community, the people who decided they were going to be catechumens had to prepare for the mystery of Baptism. They publicly proclaimed themselves catechumens, and for the next forty days they were taught the truths of this mystery, of what was going to happen to them. They were taught the mystery of the dying of Jesus Christ and of His rising, and they were led up to the point where they would sacramentally be plunged into His death on Easter Saturday night. They would be baptized by being plunged into the water, buried with Christ, as St. Paul says, in Baptism. ✍ They began to live within the mystery of water, in the presence of water, so that in choosing to be buried in the water of baptism they would be choosing life, and they would know what this choice meant for them. ✍ You and I have already been buried with Christ in Baptism. For us, Lent is a journey back into our own Baptism, but this too involves a real choosing of our true self. Maybe better than any previous culture, we realize that the self is not just the conscious part of us. We realize that there are depths within depths in all of us, and that things happen to us of which we are not conscious, and which we must recover later in conscious reflection. Our self is a deep, layered reality, and to get through the illusions and reach the true self, we have to reflect on what has happened to us. ✦ We come back to Moses, the choice of life or death and the covenant—because Baptism is our entrance into the covenant in Jesus Christ. A covenant is a reality created out of freedom. Husbands and wives covenant with one another and create their marriage, a reality which is greater than either of them. There are even much less formal covenants. Professors and students enter a covenant to love the truth, and they create a community of lovers of the truth. ✦ Covenants come out of freedom. The covenant of which baptism is the sign comes out of God's freedom and our freedom, and creates the reality of the Body of Christ. ✦ All covenants involve a sign, a promise and a demand. If you allow your life to be organized in hope of the promise, if you allow the moments of your life to be collected around the

symbol, and if you allow your own freedom to be constrained and shaped by the
demands of the covenant, you will be in
the presence of the God of that Covenant. There is a covenant with Noah, a
covenant with Moses, a covenant with
Abraham, and finally a covenant with Jesus. God says to Noah in this ancient story,
if you allow the sign of the rainbow, when
it appears, to collect your own memories
around it, if you acknowledge yourself to
be a moral being in the world capable of
choosing between good and evil, and if
you allow yourself to hope for life in a
world where life is continually threatened—
if you allow that kind of organization of
your life to take place, you will experience
the God of Noah.   ⚜   But there is a
different covenant, a different presence of
God, for Jesus. The sign of the covenant
in Jesus is Baptism. If you allow the times
of your life, the moments of your life, all
the different parts of your life to be organized over and over again by the sign of
Baptism, your own or other people's, reminded of what you're about, what you
will come to is hope in the promise of the
Resurrection.   ⚜   The life that was prom-

ised to Noah and to the people with him was the life of *survivors*. It was the life that survived the flood. The life that is promised as a hope to people who enter the waters of Baptism is *not* the life of survival, but the life that is recreated out of death. ✒ If you're looking to discover how your life can bring you into the presence of the God of Jesus, where you can choose life rather than death, don't look in the good places in you. Look in the places in you which are dead. There are places in you, there are enthusiasms that you have had, five, ten, twenty years ago that are dead. There are things that other people have done to you that have killed something in you. There are places among us as a people, as a society, that are dead. There are possibilities that existed in your life that you missed, and now they are gone, are empty, are dead. ✒ If you're looking for the God of Jesus, look among the dead with the hope of the Resurrection. See—it's not simple when you hear, "I put before you life and death. Choose life." There are layers and layers and layers of meaning to it. Not abstract theoretical meanings, but the lay-

ers and layers of meanings that are in any
human life. ✒ In what wilderness of
yourself do you wander this Lent to be
tempted between death and life, between
hope in the Resurrection or despair of the
Resurrection for yourself and for others,
reminded that at the Easter vigil you will
be confronted again with the sign of the
covenant of Jesus Christ, the water that is
the presence of the death and Resurrection of Christ?

The reason we repeat over and over again, "Christ is risen, He is truly risen," is that there isn't anything else to say. Those words are the entrance to reality. To say that Christ is risen is to express what is real. The statement of the Resurrection, as I said yesterday about the mystery of the Cross, is a cosmic statement, not a statement about some level of experience easily available to us psychologically. It's a statement about what *is*. The Scriptures (Acts 10: 34, 37–43, Col 3: 1–4, Jn 20: 1–9) tell us tonight that what *is* is Resurrection and not death, that evil is not final, but is part of the story of the love that transforms evil. The easiest way to get a sense of this kind of statement is to think about a statement that would in some ways be its own opposite. Suppose we said to one another tonight that reality is absurd, that finally there is no meaning, that finally death is ultimate and that evil is the last word. Suppose we said that. We still would not be talking about our own lives. You'd still have to decide and discover what your life means within such a world. Suppose

149

we said, as many people who are our con-
temporaries feel they have discovered, that
sorrow is ultimate and so is absurdity. Suppose we said that. What would your life
mean then? 🖋 The Word of God has
just been proclaimed: resurrection is the
ultimate truth. Our task is still to relate
that statement about reality to our own
freedom. What does your life mean if there
is resurrection from the dead? That the
Anointed One is risen is a statement about
reality: about myself, about this place,
about my body, about my own evil. 🖋
The second part of the statement is not
just a repetition: "He is truly risen." You
could say that life has meaning beyond
death in the manner of immortality, that
there are some things in human life that
are worthy enough to survive death, some
kinds of truth, beauty and love that by
their own energy or reality go beyond
death. How far beyond it we don't know,
but they go beyond it. That's *not* what
this is saying. This is not saying there is
something that escapes death. "Christ is
risen" is cosmic and general. "He is truly
risen" says that the One who rose is the
One who died. The Gospel is not saying

that there are some things in your life and in mine that are worth being immortal— some moments, some acts of love or some good things done. It *is* saying that he who was condemned to die *rose*. ✒ Now here is a further question for your freedom tonight and far beyond tonight. What does it mean to the things in you and me that will surely die to say that there is resurrection for those things? This question to your freedom, to your sense of your own meaning, to the meaning of the times in which you live is more complex and goes further and deeper than the statement that there is life beyond death, that there is meaning and not just absurdity. We are now saying (and that's why the second part of this is really the revolutionary, the humanly mad, part), "He is truly risen." ✒ The only place where you can raise these kinds of questions, where you can let this become a question which uncovers the truth of your own freedom, is the place of prayer. Prayer is a search through words and silence (sometimes with great strength, often with great doubt and fear) for resurrection. It is the acting out of the hope of our resurrection. It is lived, as the hope of the resurrection is lived, in the mystery of death. ✒ I'm not talking just about the prayer which is a movement away from your involvement with things and with your own experience. I'm also talking about the repossession of the experiences of your life in prayer and especially the living of the experiences of dying in your life, and the experiences of your own evil in the radical hope which is prayer. The One who rose from the dead is the One who became sin for us, as St. Paul says, and failed and died. That is not a statement meant to be grasped on some level of emotional experience or conscious imagery. It is a statement about what reality *is* and it raises questions about our own freedom and our own death. "Christ is risen. He is truly risen." The good news of the resurrection can only be heard by us in the places of our own death.

All of the stories in Scripture are in a way stories of Resurrection. The Gospels are not meant to be arguments to convince you about the truth of something, any more than they are meant to be biographies. They have to do with the deepening of the reality of belief, of the experience of living in the world as a believer. They describe various ways in which, within the textures of a human life, you may find yourself in the presence of the Risen One. They were written out of the experience of the Resurrection. The first stories that they told were Resurrection stories. Then they rethought all of the things that had happened between them and Jesus, and realized how those events were already an encounter with the mystery of the Resurrection, with the Triune God, finally revealed in the raising of Christ from the dead. ⚡ So you find St. Paul saying this startling thing, that the Jews leaving Egypt were already in the presence of Christ, were in the "presence of the rock, and the rock was Christ." Historically, this wouldn't make any sense at all, but with the vividness of poetry he makes the point that they were already living the mystery of the Resurrection. ⚼ Today we hear two stories, one from the Old Testament (I Sm 3: 3–10), one from the New Testament (Jn 1: 35–42), both of which have to do with beginnings. In most of the circumstances of our life we have a powerful instinct to remember the first times. People do this with their love for one another, go back to the beginnings of it, sometimes sadly, most times happily. You go back and think about what it was like when you first started being a student or started doing anything, to touch again that freshness and power and upsurge of what you are now. ⚼ Old friends talk about what it was like when the friendship began. You go back and remember what it was like when you first started imagining the sort of life you're living now. When other people begin to do what you have been doing for a long time, you get a terrific boost because through them you're in touch again with the fresh first moment. It's one of the reasons why people like kids; old timers like to see people beginning a profession; people love brides. Times of beginnings.

🌿 Why do I talk about this in reference to the place of the Resurrection in the New Testament? I'm not trying to suggest that this human love of beginnings will give us a clue to understanding the mystery of Resurrection, but rather that it gives a suggestion about how ordinary things can become the places where we first begin to hear the story of Resurrection as the word of God. 🌿 It has to do with that in us which is creative, fresh, life-giving. It has to do with us as lovers: that in myself which is a gift to love in all kinds of circumstances. It's going to be as true in the long and often dreary and not very clear middle sections of life as it is at the time of optimism and power and being close to that very first upsurge which reveals something about loving, whether it's loving a person or loving a life's work, loving an idea. 🌿 *You* as a gift of loving in the circumstances of your life right now. The re-discovery of yourself as a lover, as a gift of love in some way in your life right now, this passage of Scripture reminds you, is where you are encountering what the first Christians encountered in the mystery of the Resurrection. It's one

155

of the crucial places. That's why that second reading makes it so dramatic. Your very body is the presence of God. And your "body" doesn't just mean this physical thing: it means your history, story, your life, the things you drag along with you, the aromas of your past experience. But we've got to go still further, because that is not yet the truth of it. ✒ Suppose you were to tell the story of beginnings. You could tell a story about people who got some ideas and started off to be or do something. But in none of these people does the beginning come out of them alone. Their love, in no case, comes from suddenly getting the idea to love. It's always in the nature of a response. They're *called*, as we say. The love is called up out of them by one another, by some need or dream. ✒ The place that you can begin to hear of the Risen One, where you're in the presence of the mystery of the Father in the world, is where you are awakened to love by being loved. This is not at all an easy place to reach. It's not some aspect of ourselves, something about us that is lovable and gifted. ✒ In fact, the way to find the place of our being loved is often a passage through what in us is un-lovable and failed. It is the place in us which is the place of prayer—and all of us know how rare it is really to find ourselves there! But everyday, and in all sorts of ordinary ways it is suggested to us that we are loved. Infinite, creative Being loves you. ⚡ One key place for this most important discovery of being loved—a discovery which opens the possibility of hearing the word of the Resurrection—is in our own loving. Remember the stories about beginnings? We realize our own loving is a response, a gift. ⚡ You live the reality of your own life, not always clearly, certainly not always with confidence, often having to bear the complexity and paradox of what your *self* is, which is much harder to bear than the complexity and paradox of other people. Living your life as one who is loved. Living within the reality of that love though it very often is not clearly seen. ⚡ It's not surprising that this should be hard for us to think about or understand because we're talking about the reality that Christ discovered in the un-understand-able mystery of death. The discovery that He was loved. That even there He was in

the presence of love. To come to regard
ourselves as the Father regards us, with
love. Not just those parts of ourselves that
are worth loving, but our *selves.*
Where do you begin to hear of the mystery of the Resurrection? Where are you,
where am I, in the presence of this truth
of reality? In ourselves as the gift of love,
but deeper than that, *within* that but
deeper, maybe more painfully, certainly
needing more hope and courage and
imagination in *ourselves as loved.*

The best expression of the mystery of the Ascension is that line of St. Paul's (Eph 1: 22–23), "He has put all things under His feet and made Him as the ruler of everything, the head of the Church which is His body." And especially this part, "The fullness of Him who fills the whole creation." You notice immediately that the Ascension is in some ways the most mystical of the Christian feasts. It is one of the mysteries in expressing Christianity which comes closest to the affirmation of mystical experience in all religious traditions. ⚜ What is expressed in the mystery of the Ascension of Christ is the closing of the circle. The closing of the circle, first of all, in the journey of the Divine Son into human history: his becoming man, his taking of a human nature, his living the radical estrangement that is within human history, the loneliness, the isolation, the domination by death and sin; his living that, and his finding within that, through love, through obedience, a path back to the Divine. ⚜ The closing of the circle. The Son who became man, now truly man, becomes intimately part of the reality of God. There is no longer, really, any distance between God and us other than the metaphysical distance between Creator and creature. There is no distance between God and human beings. Human nature is, in the nature of Jesus, transformed in the mystery of Resurrection. God and human beings are perfectly one. The circle is closed. ✍ And so we can say something about Jesus which is, properly speaking, only to be said about God. He is everywhere. The fullness of Him who fills the whole creation. ✍ The Ascension is the affirmation of what all mystics have experienced, the communion, the unity, the near-identity, between the Holy and myself. It's also a feast of intimacy in another direction because not all of time and all of history has closed the circle. The man Jesus did, but not the rest. So there's a movement still going on of all human reality toward our destiny of identity with God. It was the work of the man Jesus. It is now ours. The crucial thing he says is, "As I was sent, I now send you." "I can forgive, you can forgive." "I could overcome death, you can overcome death."

🖋 We are to become the Body of Christ in the space and time of our lives, with whatever is in it, whatever disappointments or successes or any of the rest of it—in the time of our lives we are to become the Body of Christ: human reality is moving closer to its destiny or not, depending on what we do. 🖋 The feast of the Ascension is a feast about the intimacy between people and between human beings and God. Within the life of God now, there is no separation between human nature and the Divine nature: they are completely one. Within our lives now there is no separation between what we are living and the act of God entering the world to join it to Himself. We are now Christ's body in this space and time.

In the Image of God

Rev. Robert S. Smith is a priest of the Diocese of Rockville Center, New York. Since his ordination in 1958, he has served as a Professor of Philosophy in the Diocesan Seminary, as a Campus Minister at several universities on Long Island, and is presently Chaplain to the staff of University Hospital at Stony Brook.